PRAISE FOR *DOES CHANGE HAVE TO BE SO HARD*

"Does Change Have to Be So Hard is a fabulous book which provides a comprehensive understanding of how your mind works to keep you from achieving your dreams. Julie does a wonderful job offering simple and powerful strategies. This is a must-read!"

—Marcia Wieder,
America's Dream Coach, CEO/Founder, Dream University®

"Julie Donley provides us with an inspiring step-by-step approach to change as she nurtures our success as only Julie can. Often,, the desire for change is met with a wall of not knowing where to even begin. This wall immobilizes us. In *Does Change Have to Be So Hard* Julie provides us with a starting place, outlines a process to lead us through the physical and emotional aspects of successful change, and supplies the 'right thinking' so we can create lasting change and dispute the unhealthy thinking that impedes our progress. Thanks, Julie, for helping us to take change from Hard to Easy!"

—Mikki Funderburke, RN,
Owner, BestChoiceChanges

"Powerful, practical, and easy to read, *Does Change Have to Be So Hard* goes straight to the heart of where people live. Julie's candid wisdom, forged from her own life experiences, takes the fear out of change, and replaces it with empowering actions and insights. If you want to turn a page in your life, take it easy for a change—let the pages in this book guide you to success."

—Peter D Demarest, coauthor,
Answering the Central Question:
How Science Reveals the Keys to Success in Life, Love, and Leadership

"When it comes to change, Julie Donley is a true authority. As one of Julie's clients, I can personally attest to her ability to bring about positive change in your life. I began working with Julie in the middle of the infamous real estate crash. My business income decreased 47 percent that year and 30 percent the year before. Money problems brought more stress, health problems, and a lack of direction. Something had to CHANGE. I needed to change my attitude, focus, and strategy for future success in a new market. With Julie's help I inspected many facets of the way I thought and what I valued. We focused on change, and she made it EASY! My last two years have seen 30 percent to 40 percent increases each year. Even better though is that my life is more balanced, and I get much more enjoyment out of living.

"In this book, you get Julie's expert advice on how to make positive changes in your life. Here she provides a step-by-step guide that if you follow will guarantee success. The book is even EASY to read and includes personal and real-life examples that you can relate to."

—Scott Saghirian,
Associate Broker, Keller Williams Select Realtors

"That is life: things change. *Does Change Have to Be So Hard* openly examines the phases of change, from resistance to acceptance, and redefines how making successful changes in one's personal and professional life can be accomplished. Donley not only openly discusses how 'life has its own pace,' she also compassionately challenges the reader to accept that change too has its own pace and to 'accept where you are at the present moment.' Not a path of instant gratification, the author explores the factors, motivators, and de-motivators of change. Using her life as an example, Donley candidly and humbly discusses how fears, habits, and needs can be an anchor in moving toward easy, or at least easier. She gently urges you to take an honest assessment of self and situation—a necessary step toward successful transformation. 'We all need someone to believe in us.' Through her positive yet pragmatic guidance, it is evident that Julie Donley believes in the reader and champions the idea that change is always possible."

—Astrid Schmidt, Esq.,
Director, Law Career Development Office,
University of Baltimore School of Law

"*Does Change Have to Be So Hard* by Julie Donley is a great read for anyone wanting to make some change in their personal life. Being committed to change and picturing the change you want will help keep you focused until the new behavior you were trying to achieve becomes more natural for you. Staying focused on results and being intentional with the strategies will help you be successful. The book is written with compassion and understanding and helps us have courage to take the necessary steps to make such powerful changes in our life. You can see that Ms. Donley's years of experience as a psychiatric nurse have given her great insight into the many challenges people face and the great difficulty they have in seeing themselves any different. I thoroughly enjoyed this book. Thank you."

—Cheryl Hubbard,
Senior Director, Learning & Conferencing,
United Way Worldwide

"Life is inherently unmanageable. If you seek to control it, you leave yourself susceptible to exhaustion, depression, and addiction. Change is the essence of living. Learning to navigate change in a positive direction will deepen your capacity to live freely. Within these pages is a 'hope-filled' approach to spiritual and personal growth. Full of wisdom, alluring, and profound . . . it will take you to a freer level of mind. An important contribution, beneficial and insightful to everyone. Open this book with a journal, pen, and highlighter . . . as you will return to these words again."

—Marc Aldrich, BA,
Mental Health Technician

"Julie's book is like a chat over a cup of tea; warm, comfortable, energizing, and uplifting. She understands and empathizes with all people in their daily walk through life. She shares her wisdom gleaned from years of formal education and personal experiences to guide us in our own lives of constant change. Her book is a must-read for all people who work with other people. It is especially recommended for educators in understanding and motivating students."

—Marcia Luebbe, MSEd,
Curriculum and Assessment Coordinator

"Julie Donley offers practical advice that anyone can use to make the changes you desire in your life. Through sharing her own story and the stories of others, Julie highlights the four barriers to change and provides insight into why we find it hard to change. Then, step by step, she offers eight strategies to help facilitate change in your life.

"This book empowers you through knowledge plus specific strategies to change your habits and your mindset and helps you to see what motivates you and what holds you back. Especially important are the sections on releasing old habits and old thinking patterns. Julie's strong and encouraging support throughout these pages assists you to identify what you want and successfully make hard changes become easy changes."

—Karyn Greenstreet, Small Business Coach

"There are few of us who have reached the 'age of consent' who have not loudly proclaimed, 'YES, world, I consent to live here' BUT . . .' In Julie Donley's remarkable and cleverly written tribute to living with change, you will quickly recognize your hopes, your dreams, your fears, and your tears neatly bundled for that long awaited 'Aha moment.' Beginning with page one, *Does Change Have to Be So Hard* offers a concise and recognizable easy read for taking the steps needed to be present, practical, productive, and powerful through life's many passages. READ IT, LIVE IT, and GIVE IT as a treasured gift."

—Delba Riddick,
Cancer Survivor, Senior Nonprofit Executive

"Julie Donley understands how to make changes in life and knows how difficult that can be. She uses examples from her own life to illustrate what it takes to change, what causes failure, and what to do instead that leads to success. In her new easy-to-read book, *Does Change Have to Be So Hard*, Julie guides readers through eight interconnected strategies for making lasting change in any aspect of life one chooses. She makes living the life one has dreamed of seem possible and gives readers the tools needed to turn those dreams into reality. I should know . . . she guided me to do the same, and I'm living proof that anyone who is willing to commit to the changes they want to make, take action no matter what the challenge, fend off discouragement and disappointment when they occur, celebrate small wins along the way, and believe in themselves by taking one step at a time can't help but accomplish the goal they set out to achieve. If that sounds like the kind of life you would like to live, this book is for you."

—Mary O'Connor, Executive Coach

Does
CHANGE
Have To Be So
HARD

Does CHANGE Have To Be So HARD

Eight Mindset Strategies to Overcome Self-Sabotage and Take Control of Your Life

---

DR. JULIE DONLEY

CONTENTS

PREFACE

Early in 2012, after initially writing and publishing this book, I took a full-time position as a leader in a healthcare organization. Although I had been working as a solopreneur for over a decade, I felt ready and prepared to return to corporate life. The position was in behavioral health where I served as the director of nursing for a large residential treatment facility serving children and adolescents. I had been working in psychiatric nursing since early 1993 and have a passion for working with the adolescent population. I was excited for this opportunity.

It was not an easy role, and it required a lot for me to adjust to working for an organization again with different rules and structure and teams. My life had changed drastically.

Whenever you make a change in your life, you learn what you are made of. This executive position tested my strength, resilience, and leadership abilities. I was again reminded of how important personal leadership is to being a good leader. You cannot lead others well if you cannot lead yourself well.

As I revisited this book to update contact information and refresh the content as appropriate, I realized just how much of this content I had been utilizing in my leadership role. There were constant changes from embracing the responsibilities and challenges of leading others, creating a powerful and productive nursing team, changing the workplace culture, to even letting go of the role when it was time to move on. Not only did we experience changes, but I also had to initiate many changes over the years that required me to assist others in navigating through those changes successfully.

I have since returned to full-time self-employment as an executive coach and facilitator and have entered a new phase of life as I experience several life transitions. Our kids are grown, my parents need more assistance, and my husband is looking ahead to retirement. Reviewing the content in this book helped me realize some important things to make these changes easier. For example, I have been committed to living and to working a certain way, and now, I realize my priorities have shifted. My focus is no longer about raising kids and striving for achievements, but rather enjoying what I have, enriching my relationships, prioritizing my health, and giving back by helping others and sharing my wisdom. Rereading this book helped me identify areas that I want to modify and commitments that will need to change to make the experience more enjoyable and satisfying as my life shifts course.

For us to grow and become better versions of ourselves, especially as leaders, we must consider how we show up as individuals. This includes how we manage all the personal stuff—finances, health, addictions, fitness, relationships—in addition to the professional challenges. This book focuses on how to create change in your life by teaching you what to expect when you embark on a change so you understand how the mind fights to maintain the status quo. Then, you will learn strategies for making change just a little bit easier.

My first book, *The Journey Called YOU: A Roadmap to Self-Discovery and Acceptance*, helps you learn to be more self-aware, accept yourself without judgment, and make decisions that honor yourself. This is where you start to find your path to success so you can lead your best life and then help others do the same. Although people may try to skip the step of personal development and focus attention on helping others, in order to succeed at life and leadership, you must start with leading yourself.

When you understand the process of change and are able to use the strategies in this book to help make change easier for you to manage, then you can take that learning and use it when there are changes in the workplace. Once you become familiar with your experience as you go through change, you will become better at noticing and addressing things as others go through the experience of change. You will understand what is happening with others as you witness them move through the emotions related to change including denial, bargaining, anger, depression, and acceptance. You will be better equipped to navigate when others struggle with their habits, attachments, resistance, fears, and discouragement. Once you understand the brain and how it functions when the routine or status quo is threatened, you can help others prepare and travel through those tricky emotional states.

I had a really good time revisiting this work and continue to use the strategies to help me address personal and professional changes. I hope you enjoy the book and find it helpful as you navigate changes in your life.

All the best,

Dr. Julie Donley

DrJulieDonley.com

INTRODUCTION

Hard or easy, it's how you think about it.

Change is hard. If it wasn't, no one would be unhappy or stressed about change when it occurred. If we were unhappy, we would simply face the truth about our situation and make the change. It would be easy—no problem.

But change is hard, and there are reasons why change is hard. To set out on a new path and sustain a personal change where you become someone new is very challenging. It takes time, effort, and persistence. Even when it is something you really want and are dedicated to achieving, it's still hard. There are many unknown variables, and whenever you step into unknown territory, fear creeps in because of a loss of control and feelings of powerlessness. No one likes to feel like they have no power.

You're unhappy. You want something different in your life, but you don't do anything to change your situation. You think about it a lot but can't seem to take the steps required to act.

Perhaps you want a divorce. Perhaps you have been alone for a long time, and you decide you want to find a life partner. Perhaps you want to change careers, delegate more, or get promoted. Or have a baby, go back to college, get out of debt, lose weight, or quit smoking.

Why is it that sometimes we will do anything and everything it takes to get what we want while other times we get lost in the confusion of our thoughts and do nothing?

Often, there are things we know are bad for us, but we continue to do what we've always done. We don't change. Why is it easier to accept unhappiness and a life of mediocrity leading to regret and depression than to do what we must to make a better life for ourselves? Why is it such a struggle? Why must it be so *hard*?

There are times, however, when something shifts inside you, and you become willing to make a change in your life. It's as if a light switch was turned on, and you are ready to do whatever it takes. In these times, you tackle change vigorously without hesitation, doubt, or fear. You seem to be driven by an insatiable need to succeed.

But what is that light switch, and how can we turn it on so that we can proactively change things in our lives?

What makes us ready and prepared to change our lives—to change ourselves? And how might we embrace the process so that we can make change easier?

The Power to Change

In the formative years of my career, I worked as a nurse in a psychiatric hospital and then later as a nurse executive. I have studied human behavior and leadership for nearly three decades and have been a personal leadership coach for twenty years. Throughout my career, I have witnessed the power of transformation and the joy that people experience when they make a personal change—from being addicted to thriving in recovery; from being miserable at work to recognizing and maximizing their talents; from living in fear to being confident and self-assured; from being totally overwhelmed and anxious to feeling peaceful and enjoying life.

I am humbled by the personal development and growth that takes place when a client finally leaves a toxic work environment for a healthier situation or a spouse finally musters the courage to leave an empty or abusive marriage and begin a new life, moving away from what is known to making a life alone—perhaps for the first time. Or when a client learns self-acceptance and opens their heart, finally allowing love to enter as they embrace a lifelong companion.

In more recent years, as I work with leaders who wish to be more confident, more effective, and less stressed, I am a witness to the power that we can access when we move through personal change and become better versions of ourselves. As leaders evolve and grow themselves, they learn to enjoy their work and become more capable of helping others to thrive as well, and they create high-functioning and collaborative teams.

I believe that each of us has more personal power than we know how to use—and it scares us. We have the power to change our lives for the better, but we hide the best of ourselves behind a wall of fear, self-doubt, and negative mental conditioning. In order to change, to make the impact we want to have in this lifetime, we must bring down that wall to release our power, start believing in ourselves, and create powerful habits that allow us to be fully who we are.

I have always believed that we have the power to create our own happiness. My quest has been to discover those powers and learn how to use them to create a life that I love. Along the way, I have faced my share of hardships and challenges that have tested my resolve. I have had to learn to fight for life (I suffered a grave illness that nearly killed me and have been through multiple surgeries), love (my first husband and I divorced, and he died suddenly a few years later), and happiness (I've had to discover what brings me joy). I spent so many years striving to regain my health, work hard, and chase success that I had to learn how to come up for air, to do less, and to find fun as an adult. My life had become hard as a single mother with health issues. My focus was on getting it right as a mom and as a professional. To me, however, a successful life is not only about those two roles; I also had to learn how to play. Filling ourselves up with things that bring us joy enables us to have the strength to handle everything else.

Often the most difficult and challenging moments of our lives are the best teachers. The obstacles and bumps in the road I have experienced have helped me grow strong as I pushed forward despite them and learned to rise above my difficulties, conquer my fear, and overcome self-doubts.

What I have learned is that the path to happiness is easier than we think it is; we are just not very skilled at it. And because we listen to others moan and groan, we have few role models to demonstrate an easier way.

The path to happiness requires us to love, honor, and respect ourselves in every way. The more we do this, the better we become, and the happier our lives become. We are magnets of attraction. We attract things, people, situations, and resources into our lives depending upon how we think, feel, and act. So the more you respect yourself and act in ways that support you to be your best, the more you attract the things you want. And when you respect yourself, when you take actions that honor your highest self, you start to repel things you don't want, like drama, problems, and difficult people.

This concept describes the Law of Attraction, which I prefer to refer to as the Law of Attractiveness. Why? Because in order to attract what you want into your life—and repel the things you don't—you focus on becoming "attractive," so you become a magnet for your goal. Being attractive means that you possess and demonstrate the attributes and characteristics required for that goal to be yours. In other words, you must behave accordingly.

Although you have this tremendous capacity to change your life for the better, success does not happen by chance. You have the power to transform your life—if you are willing to do the work to morph and grow yourself and go the distance. Then change is possible.

Yet we sure do give ourselves a hard time, don't we?

Change is often very rewarding—even if you go into it kicking and screaming. Through the process of change, you grow stronger and more confident. Yes, there are things you may leave behind, like people you like, places you frequent, and things you enjoy. You have to become willing to let go of what was so you can allow the new to emerge. The gains you make are worth it as you grow and become a better version of yourself.

The problem is that we become attached to things staying the same. But things don't stay the same. We just *wish* they would.

Holding on to the past does not serve us. There is something better waiting for us, but we must grab the wheel of life with both hands and go for it. Life doesn't wait, and there are no encores or repeat performances. It is the journey we take, the experiences we enjoy, the lessons we learn, and the love we share along the way that matter most.

We must learn to let go and lighten up. We must learn to take charge, stop putting up with things that do not bring us happiness and joy, and learn how to love ourselves. We need to embrace our own goodness and move through our resistance to make the changes necessary to enjoy a great life.

It's time to get more comfortable with change.

We are embarking upon a journey to understand change and to empower ourselves with the strategies and beliefs needed to accomplish even the biggest personal goals.

In Search of Easy

For the first twenty years of my adulthood, life was hard! I dealt with addiction, indebtedness, divorce, obesity, single parenthood, a grave illness, bad leadership, and three layoffs—life was hard, and I was tired of it.

One day I asked a simple question: Is it possible for life to be easy? I admit that I had no idea *how* life could be easy, but if it were possible, then I believed I could find a way. All I knew was hard! This was to be a new journey for me, and there would be many changes in store.

When life is hard everything feels heavy and burdensome. Nothing seems to be going well. It's as if your mind sees only the bad, and even when you do see the good, you feel suspicious, as if something must not be right if life is calm and easy.

Somewhere along the way, we may have learned that life is supposed to be difficult and challenging. There's supposed to be chaos and stress. If there's not, then something is wrong.

This is one reason people are so stressed and feel so overwhelmed. We believe that we need to do everything all at once, and in the chase for "success," we put pressure on ourselves, and life is hard. As soon as we relax and things become calm, we pile more stuff on our plate to make it hard again. We're accustomed to life being challenging and busy. We are not comfortable with easy.

Feelings of overwhelm are a barrier to successful personal change. As you evaluate all that needs to be accomplished in order to change, you become overwhelmed just thinking about it. And if you are already stressed and busy, you are not likely to embrace change. How can you possibly look for a new job when the one you have takes all your time and energy? If you want to lose weight, how can you adjust your life if you have no time to plan your meals or to work out? How often have we heard (or given) the excuse that there's just no time to do more to care for ourselves?

If life is hard, then we cannot enjoy ourselves. We cannot find happiness through busyness.

Feeling overwhelmed *de*-motivates you to change or, rather, motivates you to continue along your current path no matter how unhappy you may be. After all, change requires work. And there is comfort in the familiar. Change brings uncertainty, and uncertainty is stressful.

But why does it have to be so hard? I mean, who says that life must be this way? Whether something is hard or easy is our perception anyway, right? Isn't it possible that life could be easy and fun? I decided that it was worth it to find out and went in pursuit of easy.

First, I needed to recognize that I was used to seeing the world a certain way. In order to change, I had to envision "easy," identify the characteristics of someone who embraces life as easy, and then start living as if life were easy.

I had to confront the thoughts telling me that I couldn't or that something was hard or that it should be a struggle, and then I had to ask myself what easy would be like instead. It took a lot of attention and practice.

One challenge is dealing with other people's beliefs about how hard something is. When I started dating at age thirty-nine, people insisted that it would be hard, that all the "good ones" my age were taken. I decided to embrace the notion that it not only could be easy but that it would be easy and that he would just walk into my life if I continued to work on becoming the kind of woman that my ideal mate would love to be with. And you know what? He did! It took time, mind you—two years from the time I committed to finding a life partner to when we began dating. But I discovered along the way that there are many single people out there of all ages. It all depends upon what you believe. And you must be patient. Life has its own pace. You do not control when it will happen, only who you become in the process.

If change is hard, we will perceive it as a chore, and we won't do the work. If we want to change, then we need for change to be easier—or, at least, we need to think of it as being easy and believe it is possible.

For change to be easy (okay, easi*er*), we must learn about and understand the process we go through when we embark upon a personal change. Then we'll know what to expect and how to cope with, prepare for, and anticipate the obstacles we will inevitably face along the way.

In addition, we must learn strategies for making change easier. If we learn these strategies and how to apply them, then we can create the changes we desire, and it won't be so hard.

This book offers you a different way of approaching change. We are rethinking change and changing how change is done. This book will provide insight into how the mind works and will present you with valuable strategies needed to approach change from a new angle. We will make it easier to achieve change as we come to understand the mechanisms involved and the forces that attempt to hold us back.

Our Journey from HARD to EASY

In this book I present you with eight strategies for embarking upon change so that it is not so difficult. But first, we must come to understand change and why we resist it. We think change is hard, and it does require effort and time for change to occur. However, the reasons we perceive change as being hard are just that, perceptions—opinions we create in our minds. Modify how we think, and we alter what we identify as "hard" to being "not so hard."

This is the essence of our journey: to learn about the mind and how it works and then learn strategies for making a change that uses the mind to support your success rather than fight your efforts, so you experience less struggle and more control, which increases your power to impact your world.

Initially, chapter 1 examines the motivations for change. You will be introduced to the four barriers to change: Habits, Attachments, Resistance, and Discouragement. These are the reasons why change is hard and often the reasons you put up with mediocrity and unhappiness. Once you understand what is really happening in your mind and how your thoughts keep you stuck, you can then use the strategies in chapters 7–14 to take charge and make the changes you want.

In chapter 2, we look at the change process and the importance of being prepared for change. If you are not yet ready for change, you will not take the actions required and you will make excuses for why you don't. This can be a huge source of frustration if you want to change but are just not yet ready mentally, emotionally, or physically. You can, however, let yourself off the hook and instead work on becoming ready and preparing yourself for the changes you wish to make. Change requires your commitment, and if you are committed to the status quo, unable to let go and take a stand for something new, you won't do the work and may beat yourself up about it. This is an internal battle not worth fighting.

Chapters 3 through 6 discuss in detail the four main barriers to successful change.

Chapter 3 reviews <u>H</u>abits and how your habits run your life. We learn about the brain and how neurological connections are formed to assist you in accomplishing tasks.

Chapter 4 looks at your <u>A</u>ttachments. No matter how uncomfortable and unhappy you may be, the brain works hard to maintain the status quo.

In chapter 5 we discuss <u>R</u>esistance, better known as fear. Fear can get the better of you. Fear rears its ugly head and tells you "No!" in many ways. Resistance shows up in your behaviors, but fear is a trick of the mind. This kind of fear is not the real fear that warns you of danger. This fear just wants to protect you, and, under this pretense, it keeps you stuck.

Chapter 6 examines how expectations set you up for <u>D</u>iscouragement and sabotage your success. You get tired. Success isn't happening fast enough. This is yet another game your mind likes to play.

As you can see already, there are reasons that change is challenging. The next eight chapters describe the strategies for making change easier and succeeding at change. And while the strategies are numbered and presented in a particular order, they can occur and be tended to in any order to help you achieve your desired outcome.

Chapter 7 introduces strategy 1: commit to change. Decide you want something different and commit to doing whatever it takes to create it. By committing to the creation of something new, you accept that the way you've been behaving will need to change. You go in search of and learn new ways of behaving and operating in life. You question how you do things now, and if they do not add value to your new life, then you easily let them go. You are committed to a new life.

Chapter 8 explains strategy 2: envision a better future. Instead of doing battle with your habits, envision a future so compelling that it becomes a guiding light to show you the way. By concentrating on your vision and taking actions that move you toward creating that vision, you easily develop new habits, and the old ones become extinct.

Chapter 9 describes strategy 3: develop the characteristics you need to succeed. In your vision for change, you are a different person with different values and priorities. You are playing a different role in relation to this change and the people in your life. Identify these characteristics and begin to develop them so that you can become the new person you need to be in the new landscape you envision for your future.

Chapter 10 explains strategy 4: create an environment to support the change. This means having the right support systems in place, such as a community of people who believe in you and can keep you focused, who keep you out of your sabotaging thoughts, and who offer new perspectives. It also includes creating a physical environment that is conducive to the change you wish to make.

Chapter 11 presents strategy 5: take action. Without action, nothing changes.

Chapter 12 introduces strategy 6: celebrate your success along the way. When you give yourself recognition for the steps you are taking and the results you are achieving, you begin to gain confidence and momentum, and this reinforces your commitment to your vision. In this way, you avoid feelings of discouragement.

Chapter 13 explains strategy 7: laugh and enjoy the journey. As you laugh, you lighten up and learn to enjoy yourself. Happiness is a key element for success because if you are not able to enjoy yourself along the journey, how will you know happiness when you arrive at your destination? What is happiness but a state of mind? If this change is a chore, you won't do it, you won't follow through, and you won't have any fun. Laughter is an essential element to tame your fear and motivate you to the finish line.

Chapter 14 reviews strategy 8: adopt empowering beliefs. Believe in the possibility of your change becoming reality, believe in yourself and the power you have to do the work, and set your intention for success. If you do not believe it is possible, if you do not believe that you can achieve success, then you will not commit and you will not follow through; in fact, you won't even bother to get started. Whatever you believe is what you will create in reality.

In the concluding chapter, I pull it all together, give you food for thought, and provide you with next steps.

My hope for you as you read this book is that you come to understand how your mind plays games with you. It doesn't mean to hold you back from experiencing the happiness you desire; that is an unintended result. By using these strategies, you will feel comfortable embarking on change and empowered to take the actions needed to make your dreams come true. These strategies will help you to become better at playing the game of change so that you increase your odds of winning. You no longer do battle with your mind; rather, you work with your mind to move you forward to become the person you wish to become, create the changes you wish to make, and enjoy the journey.

My wish for you is that learning about the mind along with these strategies helps you to navigate through the changes in your life, so you experience the love, happiness, and success you desire with less effort and stress.

CHAPTER 1

GET ACQUAINTED
WITH CHANGE

---

*"If you want to make your dreams come true, the first thing
you have to do is wake up."*

—J. M. Power

Change Is Constant

Change is happening all the time. You wake up in the morning and get out of bed. From your lying position, you are now standing. You take a shower. Now you are wet. You get dressed. You go to the kitchen. You are hungry. You eat. Now you are full.

Change is happening all the time, and we pay no attention to it. You go to work. You attend a meeting. You return to your desk. The phone rings, and you have a conversation. You finish the phone call and start working on an email. You leave at the end of the day.

Change. Small transitions occur all day, every day. You are a master at change and don't even know it. How about that?

Personal Triumphs

Of course, the little changes you manage every day are quite different than when you embark upon a big personal change. But you've done that too. Consider your own personal triumphs. We all have them. Each of us has overcome personal challenges and created great change in our lives. You may have earned a degree, quit smoking or some other addiction, gotten out of debt, moved away from home, bought a house, started a business, been promoted, changed careers, gotten married, or had kids. We have all achieved much success!

Often, we overlook these personal challenges and great feats. We take them for granted and don't acknowledge our accomplishments. We achieve great things without considering the sacrifices we had to make and all the things we had to do in order to make our dream come true.

There is a place we get to—mentally and emotionally—where we are ready for change, and we make it happen. We are focused and engaged. Directed. Determined. And we do it! We make it happen.

Then there are times when we really want change or we think we want a change, but for whatever reason, we don't get off our duffs. We struggle in our minds as we battle between our desire and the lack of motivation and the lack of action. We continue to put up with mediocrity and inaction, often beating ourselves up mentally for not changing, for not doing something different, and our self-esteem takes quite a beating. We may struggle for years to meet our ideal mate, write that novel, complete that degree, or get that promotion.

We struggle, and no matter how we try, success is elusive.

There are things we do when we are successful at change that we don't do when there is struggle and success eludes us. It's time we stopped fooling ourselves or playing games. If we want something new in our lives, then we have to find new strategies for achieving success.

If you are not yet ready to change, then focus your energies on getting ready and stop beating yourself up and giving yourself a hard time. Change comes in stages. We prepare for change in stages. We get glimpses of something we want, but we're not yet ready to take the leap. And it's okay. Accept where you are at the present moment.

Of course, if you are in a dangerous situation and you are not yet ready to change, then you may need professional help. Take responsibility for the quality of your life. No one else will. At the end of the day—at the end of your last day—it is *you* who you must answer to for the quality of your life.

Change is H.A.R.D.

Change is hard for several reasons. The acronym H.A.R.D. helps us to understand these reasons so we can appreciate the hurdles we will need to face in order to embark upon a personal change. H.A.R.D. stands for Habits, Attachments, Resistance, and Discouragement. Let's explore how each of these gets in the way of creating personal change.

Habits

What you do right now is a habit. You behave in a certain way in order to produce the results you receive. Even if you are unhappy with the results, you continue along this path because it is easier than trying to figure out a new path. Everything is automatic—you don't have to think too much about it because you've been doing things this way for so long. There is little to no effort expended to perform the tasks because this is how you've operated for years.

Along with habits of behavior, you have habits of thought and belief. Your perceptions about life, your outlook, and your view of yourself are all ingrained habits of thought. These thoughts guide your behavior. For change to take place, your belief system needs to change. You can no longer trust your own thinking. That's not an easy pill to swallow.

Attachments

You believe in the way things are. You are attached to doing things the way you've been doing them. You have thoughts and ideas about how your life should be, and you are committed to the direction you have been following all this time.

To change would mean you must first admit that your way isn't working, and most people are quite attached to their ideas. That is to say, we like to be right. To change means we would have to admit defeat, and that does not come easy. We are stubborn in our thinking. Once we admit our way doesn't work, we have to find new ways of doing things. We don't always know how to do that, so we must ask for help, which is not something that comes easy for many of us. We struggle with our not knowing and with other people telling us what to do.

Change requires a new focus, new beliefs, and disengagement from the current way of behaving in favor of a new path full of unknown variables. That's *hard!*

And it's scary.

Resistance

Resistance is fear. You resist doing what you know is good and healthy for you because you're scared. Scared of something new. Scared you won't know what to do, afraid you won't be able to handle it or go the distance. Scared of what it will mean when things are different—how other people will behave and what it will mean for you. You get scared of what other people will say or think of you, scared of being rejected by people you love, scared of losing what you have now, and scared of losing control.

You procrastinate and doubt yourself. You judge yourself harshly and question your worthiness to have something better. Fear impacts your self-esteem, so you resist; you freeze, or you fight. What you know now is at least familiar.

With change, everything gets turned upside down and backward, which feels very uncomfortable and scary, until, of course, you become accustomed to it, and it becomes second nature (a new habit).

Discouragement

Getting comfortable with the new change takes time—so very long—and we humans have trouble thinking long term. We are very short-sighted and desire instant gratification. We don't like to wait. We are impatient and expect quick results.

Also, we tend to focus on results that have not yet transpired rather than acknowledge what we have done and celebrate our successes. If all you can see is the distance you have yet to travel and never recognize how far you have come, it is quite easy to become discouraged.

Change is hard. You are stressed out at work and spend too much time there, but you don't delegate as you should and don't say no to any request. You try to lose weight, but the scale doesn't budge. You want to change jobs but don't have the energy to conduct a job search. You talk about how challenging the relationship is with your spouse or your boss or the kids, and you don't really believe change is possible. You don't see a path, so why bother?

You don't believe in yourself or trust yourself to change; it's been like this for so long. Often there are no positive people around to tell you otherwise or to teach you how or what to change. You are often not willing to learn anyway. You're not open to possibilities. You're not ready. You don't yet see the benefits of doing the work to make change possible. It's too much work, and you don't believe you will succeed. This perpetuates your pain, and you settle for what you have.

Change requires time, attention, direction, and consistency, and we generally won't hang in there long enough to do what it takes to make change happen.

Unless we are ready. Or we're forced to change.

Change by Force

Being forced to change means that there is a severe penalty or consequence that is being presented to you. A "whack on the side of the head" wakes you out of your stupor or denial and offers you few options. It's like you reach a fork in the road, and you must make a choice about your future and the direction of your life. For example, you lose your job, so you have to find a new one. You do not receive the promotion you hoped for, or you receive a poor annual evaluation, and now must reevaluate your situation. Your doctor gives you bad news about your health, so now you have to drop a few pounds, stop smoking, or give up fast food . . . or else suffer the consequences. The police pull you over suspecting you are driving under the influence (DUI); you either get help or go to jail. Your spouse is having an affair, forcing you into counseling or divorce.

Of course, there is always a choice. You could do nothing and continue to live with your cheating spouse or smoke until you die of lung cancer. You could remain out of work, lose your house and all your belongings, and go into bankruptcy. These are options should you decide to do nothing. It sounds kind of ominous, but people do make these choices. For some people, the problem is so overwhelming that they slip into denial and pretend it isn't happening or become so depressed that they do not have the ability to face their reality. Either way, change is needed, perhaps with some professional assistance.

There are times when you know you need to change and you think about it, but instead of being proactive, like decreasing your stress *before* you have a heart attack or talking to a financial planner *before* you go into foreclosure, you sabotage things. You wait until things get so bad that you are forced into action. In these instances, it takes some external force to push you into submission. You do not accept responsibility for your behavior; rather, someone or something else compels you to take action.

Force is not pretty because you don't *choose* to move forward and create something new; you *have* to or else suffer the consequences. This can often bring about feelings of anger, resentment, and powerlessness.

Change by Choice

The other option is to *choose* change. Choosing change means that you have become willing to do whatever it takes to make a change in your life. You sacrifice the comfort of the way things are in exchange for the hope and promise of something better.

Choosing change is empowering. It means taking responsibility for the direction of your life instead of waiting for the forces of fate to push you into moving and making a change. You willingly choose to take the actions needed to change course and move forward.

This isn't pretty either, because any way you look at it, change is hard. There are forces at work that are doing their best to keep you right where you are—habits, attachments, resistance, and discouragement.

But fear of consequences is also a motivator for change. If you are scared to die, and most people are, then you might be more willing to give up greasy foods as recommended by your doctor so you can continue to live and enjoy yourself, your relationships, and your work. You make a decision that it is of greater value and importance to you to live long and be active to be able to enjoy your grandkids rather than eat that fried chicken or that greasy, supersized burger. Somewhere along the way, you consciously decide that something in the future is more important to you than instant gratification. Although you may desire those fries and soft drink, your health, and the ability to enjoy your family or avoid future health problems, becomes of greater importance than the momentary satisfaction of your taste buds.

This is what I refer to as "short-term pain for long-term gain."

Externally Motivated to Change

Outside forces or trends can contribute to our willingness to embrace change. For example, George (not his real name) worked at a factory for twenty years until management announced that the factory would be closing over a period of a few years. They provided the employees with outsourcing to help people change careers and find new employment, and there was funding for education if people wanted it. George shared:

> They told us that this funding would not be available forever. "If you wanted to go to school, we'll pay for it," they said. I took advantage of the opportunity. I became an occupational therapist like my cousin, and then I went back to nursing school because the demand was high, and the money was good.
>
> The opportunity to return to school was handed to me. I was one of the youngest employees at the factory. Ninety-nine percent of the people did not take advantage of the educational opportunity.

George was externally motivated to change. If the factory had not closed or if there was no funding for school, he might have made different choices. But because of the opportunities, he saw new options for himself and envisioned possibilities for a better life. He left the factory, which has since closed, and has been practicing nursing now for eight years.

That is life. Things change. Businesses close. People get sick. People die. And we have to adjust. There are external forces that cause us to awaken to new possibilities. Or we stay stuck in nostalgia wishing things were different.

Internally Motivated to Change

Being internally motivated is something else. You have an inner drive to be better, to improve, to do something greater, to become more than what you are now.

Sometimes that switch just isn't turned on.

Sometimes your environments, both internal (that is, in your mind) as well as external (the people around you) are not supportive of you making a change. They are not nurturing you to improve or grow, be creative, or expand your horizons. There are many forces that try to keep you as you are now, the worst of which is in your own head. At least with people, situations, and external things, you can get up and leave. But *you* go with you everywhere you go! You cannot leave your mind behind.

Learning to manage your internal environment is essential for creating the changes you want in life.

To become internally motivated to change requires that you become aware of what is important to you and why you do the things you do, then choose how you want to live your life based on what you value.

For instance, often people are motivated by their needs. You have a need to impress others so you dress a certain way even though it may cause you to spend more money than you have. At some point, the switch could flip, causing you to decide that you want money to get married, have kids, or save for retirement. That becomes important to you—more important than running out to buy the latest gadget or hottest new fashion trend. Valuing your money and choosing to save rather than spend creates a shift and starts you on a new path.

Intrinsic motivation is important for success. It causes you to dig deep within for the strength and courage to face not only your fears but yourself as well. You start to see all you are capable of doing and becoming. You start to respect yourself in new ways and begin on the path of personal development. And once you begin on that path and get a taste of success, you want more and more! Intrinsic motivation is very powerful!

People have a tremendous internal capacity for motivation; we just don't know how to tap into it very well. Leaders who create positive work environments that nurture authenticity and innovation are able to unleash scads of creativity from their workers. Romantic relationships, friendships, and partnerships are able to nurture the best in their partners by providing a safe environment for the person to flourish and be themselves, hence the success of the coaching profession. There is truth in having someone on your side behind the scenes cheering for you, demanding your best, and loving you—accepting you—for who you are without judgment. We all need someone to believe in us.

But all too often we find ourselves in situations that stifle our best. We find ourselves in toxic work environments and relationships that do not nourish us. We shut down and build walls to hide our capacity and our productivity out of fear—fear of rejection or judgment, of not being accepted, or of being ridiculed. We build walls to protect us because it is a quick and simple way to stifle our emotions rather than face them and express our needs. We disdain asking for help, so we suppress our needs, run from ourselves, and allow others to beat us into submission. We succumb to mediocrity.

Choose Your Incentive: Pain or Pleasure

People endure a lot of pain without realizing it. You put up with so much stuff that you do not like, that causes you pain and frustration and aggravation. You hold tight to old wounds and repeat damaging behaviors. Day after day, you are bombarded by life's negative forces and you do battle, often without realizing just how much of a fight you are enduring—until, of course, at the end of the day when you crash from exhaustion!

You may also have difficulty being happy and enjoying pleasurable experiences. It may sound odd, but since true happiness comes from within, in a world where most people are so busy and full of worry, happiness and joy are often left on a wish list somewhere.

Change is possible.

You can learn to sensitize yourself to your pain. You can also learn how to be happy and enjoy yourself. But you cannot do either if you are moving a hundred miles an hour. You have to slow down enough to assess your life and learn about yourself—your likes, your dislikes, what makes you unhappy or uncomfortable, where you are frustrated or angry—before you can begin to change anything. You have to decide that you want something different—something better—for yourself and your life, and you have to be willing to step out of your comfort zone in order to go for it—regardless of what other people think, say, or do. In other words, you're going to have to face your fear.

The Hardest Thing to Do

On the addiction unit where I often worked as a nurse, I used to tell patients that the hardest thing they will ever do is *get* clean; it is much easier to stay clean one day at a time than it is to get there. The hardest thing to do is to get to where you are headed because you have to change everything.

- You have to admit that the way you've been doing things isn't working—not to get you to where you want to be, anyway.
- You have to let go of bad habits and all the things you are accustomed to because what you do now, how you think now, will not get you to where you want to be. You have to stop doing things the way you've always done them and adopt a "beginner's mind."

- You have to learn new things. You have to be open to listening to other people tell you new ways of thinking about and approaching whatever your goal is. I mean, if you knew how to do it, you'd be doing it and you'd already be there, right?

- You have to ask for help, do the research, find mentors or teachers, and figure out new ways of doing whatever it is you are trying to do. Most people have a difficult time admitting that they could be wrong or do not have the answer. We want to be right. We like to figure things out on our own. We hate to open up and tell others how we feel. I mean, *What will people think if they knew this about me?*

Our mind makes it tricky for us to change. In essence, you have to let go of the old and embrace something new. Well, that's *hard*! And it requires effort! And it takes time!

Who wants to work that hard? And really, who likes to wait? We want immediate results and instant gratification!

Throughout your life, you have programmed your mind and body to respond in a certain way to the triggers of daily life. It's how you operate. Now you want to change everything!? Come on! Of course you're going to resist.

Whether you want to be less stressed and burned out and learn to enjoy your work; be at peace when you were only ever focused on completing the to-do list or striving to make money; get clean when you've been addicted to drugs, drinking, sex, gambling, work, or food; lose weight when you've been heavy for many years; be happy when you've been too busy to care; start your own business or change careers when you are so accustomed to your job, miserable as you may be; fall in love and be romantic when you've been so angry—change requires that you leave behind habits of thought and behavior and beliefs that no longer work for you and create new habits that allow you to produce something new.

And it may be the hardest thing you'll ever do.

Are You Ready for Change?

"We should never be ashamed to change; we should be ashamed NOT to change."

—*Unknown*

You *say* you want to change jobs, finish that degree, be less stressed, start playing an instrument, exercise, take up a hobby, or improve your relationship with your spouse. You *say* this change would add value to your life, make you healthier, richer, happier, more peaceful . . . You need to do something because as things are you are not happy, and you know life could be better than this.

But are you *ready* to change?

You tell yourself you need to do this. You tell others too. People are tired of hearing it! And so are you!

But wanting something isn't enough to do the work. You must be ready, willing, and able to do whatever it takes to follow through and make it happen.

Although you want something different, you may not be at the point where you are willing to commit to change. This is why you keep talking about it, wanting it, and dreaming about it but are not taking the steps needed to make the change. You are not ready to commit.

Being ready requires you to do certain things:

- Surrender to your reality. Be clear about where you are right now and accept that your previous choices have gotten you here.

- Decide that this is not what you want.

- Believe that there is something better for you—of greater value and importance—and become willing to discover what that is.

- Commit to this new path—even if you are unsure what path you will take, you know that *this* is not it. You must become willing to let go of what you have in order to seek and find something better.

When you are committed, then you are ready. Until you are committed, you are still contemplating, dreaming, wishing . . .

It is okay to dream and wish for better things. We need to do that in order to identify areas of our life where we are not satisfied. Once we become aware, then we can make different choices to create something new for ourselves.

Dreaming and wishing, however, does not mean that you are ready to actually embark upon the change. It simply means you are, well, dreaming.

People who seek out a resource, such as a coach, teacher, or mentor, are ready. They want something better, are taking steps to do something about it, and want a guide or partner to help them get there, teach them what they need to know, and keep them focused and accountable. Other people seek out resources that can assist them along their journey as they dive into the change they want to make. This could be a career consultant to find a new job, a personal trainer to help with accountability for working out, or even a physician for a health evaluation. Or they may simply start taking steps toward their desired outcome on their own.

If you are not acting on your desire to change, perhaps you are not ready. Acknowledge that. Don't fight with yourself about it. Accept it. Be okay with it. It's a great place to be. It doesn't mean anything. It means you are here, not there. Instead of beating yourself up or wishing and hoping for change, focus on getting ready.

To be ready for change means you are willing to become someone new, and since you only know how to be who you are now and do the things you do, everything needs to be different. You need to learn new tools for living in order to achieve the change you want to make.

Being ready only requires that you are willing and prepared to begin. It is okay for you to not know how to proceed—at least at first. That will come.

First, get ready. And if you're not ready for change, focus your energies on getting ready.

CHAPTER 2

PREPARE FOR CHANGE

"He who fails to plan is planning to fail."

—Winston Churchill

Going on Vacation

If you were going on a vacation, you would take certain steps to prepare. You may research different places, decide on a budget, and read reviews from other people who have traveled to those destinations. You decide where you will go, when, and for how long, what you will do there, what you will take, who will go with you, what you need to know about the area, and how you will get there.

Once those things are decided, then you plan your trip, schedule time off from work, and get prepared, including packing and making arrangements for pets to be cared for, mail to be stopped or brought in, your house to be watched, and so on.

This all happens before you leave for vacation.

You get ready, you get yourself set up and prepared, and then, when the day arrives, off you go!

The same is true with change. When you want change, you first must get prepared. There is a whole process to getting yourself

15

ready: You have to decide where you want to go and make a decision to follow this path. You have to become aware of what you do now, learn a new skill set, and then practice over and over again until it becomes habit, and the old habit dies or at least lessens. You have to tap into your strengths and stop battling with your weaknesses. You need to prepare your environment for success, and you need support—too often we think we can simply go it alone. We're embarrassed, or we simply do not see the value in having someone assist us. Often the people with whom you spend the most time are not the people who will support you on this new journey. You will need a community of the right supporters and skills for managing the naysayers in your life.

If you knew what to do, you'd already be doing it. The thinking that got you here won't get you there. The behaviors you practice today have gotten you the results you have today; they won't take you to the new place you want to go. You need new thoughts and new behaviors. You will also need to believe in the possibility for success or else you will not be willing to commit to go the distance.

Change is scary because it is new. You don't know what to do, and you are uncertain as to what's on the other side of the change, so you don't know what to expect.

It's also scary because, well, it's a lot of work and it takes time. You question whether you can do it. Will you be able to follow through?

You worry about becoming overwhelmed—and rightly so, which is why asking the question of whether you are ready for change is essential. Why stress about it if you're not ready? You can simply focus your efforts on getting ready.

You Are a Master of Change

You have made great changes in your life. Consider how you arrived at your current circumstances, how you made choices to learn a trade, target a particular position, get married, or find a home. You've dealt with losses and with accomplishments. You've experienced a lot of personal changes.

You also go through change in a myriad of ways all day long as you shift from one activity to another.

Change is not the issue. You are very accustomed to change. You have routines that help you adapt to daily changes. You might drive the same way to work to smooth the change from home to the office. Break the same time for lunch to add consistency to the change from work to rest. These habits of thought or behavior patterns help you to cope with change. You don't spend a lot of time thinking about these changes; you just flow with them.

A layoff will throw you out of this routine very suddenly, as will a death or illness or even a detour from your usual route to work. It is this change that is scary because you feel as though everything is out of sorts. You have lost the routine that you counted on. It was predictable, and there was a sense of security in that predictability. You felt like you had some control. Suddenly nothing is predictable, and you feel out of control.

In reality, there is very little we have control of. We *think* we have control over many things, and we hold on very tightly. This causes stress, struggle, and frustration. If, however, we let go and focus our attention on what we can control, then we experience much less stress and actually feel much more empowered.

What Do You Control?

> *"Between stimulus and response there is a space. In that space is our power to choose our response. In our response lies our growth and our freedom."*
>
> —*Viktor Frankl*

You control you—your thoughts, feelings, and behaviors. When you become emotional, you can choose your response.

People react to their emotions without forethought. They are at the mercy of their emotions, and their emotions dictate their behavior. When you operate in this way, you give tremendous power to your primitive brain, the part of the brain that acts on instinct. While this is not bad or wrong per se, there is no censor or filter. The filter or control center is part of the new brain, the frontal cortex.

Access to this part of the brain requires that we become aware of and recognize our emotional state and pause before responding. This requires discipline and a desire to self-manage as you must remain alert, consciously checking in with yourself and your body to assess emotional messages and recognize your feelings.

Only by becoming aware of a particular feeling or mood can you then regulate or manage yourself and your actions in response. First you have to notice that you are experiencing an emotion and then name it. Emotions are data and provide you with information. Once you notice you are feeling some way, you can then inquire what that emotion is telling you.

With change, we experience many different emotions. This emotional rollercoaster is another reason we fear change. The emotions can be overwhelming, and people can have a difficult time sorting through them all.

As you go through your day and experience the little changes that occur, you pass through these emotions so briefly that you don't notice them and don't bother to pay attention.

For example, you wake up to the alarm. You are tired. You don't want to get up yet. You are disappointed because you really want to sleep more. You may be angry that you stayed up so late the night before. You might wish that you could call out sick—you may even consider it. In the end, you get up and get on with your day.

All of this might happen in a matter of seconds. Similar events occur throughout your day. You are happily making progress on a project when you have to stop what you are doing in order to attend a meeting. You become frustrated, angry, disappointed. You may stomp your feet. Swear a bit. Then you come to terms with reality and go to your meeting.

If we can predict these emotional states as we move through change and learn how to manage our emotional reactions, we can reach acceptance in less time and with less stress. Once we reach acceptance, we are empowered to take action and manage our thoughts, feelings, and behaviors with greater ease.

Three Phases of Change

Whether you know it or not, you pass through several stages, or phases, when change occurs—by choice or by force. Author William Bridges has done extensive work on transitions, especially in the workplace. I have witnessed these same phases in the situations of thousands of clients and patients—as well as in my own life. Understanding them and learning to recognize the emotions associated with them is the precursor for being able to manage your emotional state and your behavior.

Knowledge empowers you to predict what will happen, and with self-awareness, you can identify the emotion and the phase to help you move through it with less stress and pain. In this way you feel more comfortable and less fearful, and change becomes easier to manage.

Phase 1: The Ending—what *was* is over

Endings are difficult. We want to hold on to things. We want this moment to go on forever. Often the most difficult thing for people to accept is that everything in life is temporary and fleeting. We may enjoy someone or something for a short time or a long time; there is no way to know. Regardless, it just never seems to be long enough.

This is why it is important to enjoy things and people who enter our life while they are here, to be present in what is going on in this moment. Too often we are busy thinking about and wishing for other things that we miss the moment; we give up the opportunity to be with what is happening in this moment, this now. Then, when something is destroyed or lost, or someone we love dies, we want it back. We weren't finished yet!

We must focus on what we can control, which is ourselves: our thoughts, feelings, and behaviors.

With change, the ending presents you with the opportunity to let go of what was to make space for something new. You must let go and accept this new landscape—like it or not. Life will be different now. Accepting life without this person, place, thing, or situation does not mean you have to like it or agree with it. Your job is simply to embrace this new reality minus the thing lost.

With any ending, you can expect to experience the five stages of grief, as identified by the famed Swiss-American psychiatrist, Elisabeth Kübler-Ross, MD:

1. Denial
2. Bargaining
3. Anger
4. Sadness or depression and, finally,
5. Acceptance

The sooner you can come to accept your reality, the easier the transition will be for you. This is what you can control or work on to move through this phase more quickly and with greater ease:

- Recognize the emotions you are experiencing,
- Talk about them with your coach, trusted advisor, or therapist, or use a journal to work through them, and
- Move yourself toward acceptance.

You may notice that you are unable or unwilling to accept this new information about the change. People mention it to you, and you are completely closed-minded to hearing it. Nope. This cannot be happening—not to you, not now. ***This is denial.***

You may struggle because you don't want something to end, wishing you could go back in time and savor it all over again. You hear yourself wishing things were different and find yourself saying, "If only . . ." That's nostalgic. And ***that's bargaining***.

You may struggle because you had other expectations and ideas. How dare this happen now. ***That's anger***.

You may find yourself crying, feeling melancholy or withdrawn, and not talking to anyone. ***That's sadness***.

Fear underlies each of these emotions. Acknowledge your fear. What are you fearful of? List all of the things that this change causes you to fear or worry about. Take note of these thoughts. They are just thoughts, but if not acknowledged, they are likened to a subliminal message running in the back of your mind, guiding you and influencing your behavior.

Give yourself the space and time needed to enjoy your emotions as they relate to your situation. It feels good to *feel*. That is what is so special about being human. It feels good to cry when you're sad and in pain, or to be angry when you're upset about something. Feel the emotion and let it go.

There is no timeframe or time limit for grieving. You may move through the stages to acceptance and then you're sad again. Or angry. There is no right or wrong way to feel your feelings. They are yours and they are normal, and they may be different from someone else's. If you get stuck and cannot function or move on with your life after a considerable amount of time has passed, then it may benefit you to see a counselor or therapist.

One point to note: be careful about your support system during the process of mourning. Identify what you need from others and then seek out the right person with whom you can express yourself. People often struggle with knowing how to handle your emotional state, and they may not do a very good job of listening or meeting your needs. Forgive them; they just don't know how to handle mourning.

The easier it is for you to confront and then let go of these emotions and accept your reality, the easier you will pass through this phase into acceptance. Only when you accept your reality and let go of what was are you free to then move on and take steps to create something new, something wonderful.

Phase 2: The Middle—the space in between

When you are in the middle of change, you feel disoriented, scattered, and anxious. You are unsure of what is coming next. You may still feel loss over what has ended.

It is very uncomfortable to be in this place.

Characterized by feelings of disorientation and uncertainty, you feel like someone lost at sea during a storm wondering if you've packed a lifejacket. Uncertainty breeds fear.

Unfortunately, there is not much you can do during this phase other than weather the storm and go for the ride.

The problem here is not only that this phase feels uncomfortable but that there is no stability, no firm ground, and nothing to hold on to. You seem to be drifting along aimlessly, no longer part of what came before and not yet into something new.

Resist the temptation to complain. There is no amount of anxiety or worry that will enable you to rush through this phase. Accept that this is where you are right now; it will not last. Be okay with feeling uncomfortable and being in this space of unknowing. This too shall pass.

Trust and reach for your faith in knowing that you will be okay and that your next steps will become clear if you keep doing what you need to do to care for yourself. That part is essential; you must respect yourself and do what you need to do to take care of yourself.

There is no way of knowing how long you will be in this space. That means you must be patient and ride out the storm until you see land. Focus on what you can control, which is letting go of the past and envisioning your future.

Phase 3: The Beginning—what's to come

This is the exciting phase. It is where your vision for success—your dream—lives!

It is also very scary. I mean, it's not real yet. What if it doesn't happen? What if it's only wishful thinking?

Notice how I am projecting thoughts into the future, a future which is not yet here. It is a fantasy.

You don't know what the next thing will be like. You may only know that what came before is over. This unknown can cause fear, angst, and discomfort. It tests your faith that you'll be okay, that you will like whatever comes your way, and that you will be able to manage it.

Fear causes resistance. We resist change because we are scared, and our fear can paralyze us. But excitement can also show up as fear. Fear can be excitement turned inside out.

Recently, a friend mentioned that she purchased her very own motorcycle after obtaining her license. Finally, after many years of dreaming of this day. She was so excited. She climbed onto her cycle, and, suddenly, she was scared stiff. She was shaking and could barely move. She sat on it for a while, and then she and her husband put it on the trailer and drove it home.

It never occurred to her that it was excitement, not fear, that gripped her that day. This was such an important accomplishment. She had waited years to fulfill this bucket list item, and now she'd done it! She was very grateful for this revelation, and since she acknowledged this, she has been enjoying her new ride.

The focus of this phase is on dreaming and imagining what you want and how you want the outcome to look and feel. Your power to create what you want starts in your mind. You envision it first, then create it in reality. In his bestselling book, *The 7 Habits of Highly Effective People*, Steven Covey refers to this as "beginning with the end in mind."

Don't become attached to your vision or expect your vision to be reality right now—it is only a fantasy after all. It is a future possibility. Often life has other, better things in store for you. But this is where the Law of Attraction begins—thinking about and dreaming of the wonderful things you want in your life, what you'll be doing in this new landscape, and how you will feel.

The beginning also brings with it feelings of anticipation, anxiety, and impatience. There are a lot of emotions involved with change!

You may experience all three phases at once or one at a time. You could go through different changes at the same time and be in different phases for different changes, which brings on many different emotions all at once.

And at the same time, your partner, coworkers, boss, and other people in your life are experiencing different emotions related to changes going on in their lives as well as perhaps a change that is going on for all of you.

Whew! With loads of emotional energy bouncing around, you bet it's scary! People aren't skilled at navigating through emotional waters. And yet it's really awesome that we humans get to experience this wide array of emotions . . . even if we don't know how to manage them well.

There is nothing wrong with emotions. Enjoy them. Allow yourself to experience them when they arise. Recognize them and acknowledge them. They bring you a message that needs to be understood so that you can choose your response as opposed to being at the mercy of your emotional state.

You can be emotional; just don't let your emotions dictate your behavior. Use your emotions as a catalyst for action.

Being self-aware is essential. Recognizing your emotions, acknowledging them, and processing them either by talking about them with another human being or by writing in a journal will help you move through them swiftly. When you don't acknowledge your emotions, you suppress them. This doesn't make them go away, but, rather, they fill up space and take their toll on your physical health over time.

There are many studies now linking emotions with physical illness, including some cancers. Pent-up emotions can cause mental health issues too, such as clinical depression or severe anxiety, and they can interfere with your relationships and quality of life.

Reaching a Tipping Point

I started smoking when I was very young. I would love to blame it on peer pressure, but I think I was one of the first to begin. What can I say, I was a leader at a young age!

Back then, it was the thing to do. We were unaware of the dangers of smoking. This was before the lawsuits and the links to cancer. Eventually, as the dangers became known, my father began to clip out articles and give them to me.

But I was a smoker. That's how I defined myself. I never really thought about quitting. It was a habit, and I enjoyed it (or so I told myself). So, although I would peruse the articles, I was committed to smoking.

And honestly, during that time of my life, I had other priorities. I was a teen when I started and then entered early adulthood. I was trying to find myself and then my place in the world so I could make a living. I was focused on college and getting into a career.

So what changed? What caused this pack-a-day smoker for sixteen years to give it up one weekend in the summer of 1994?

Well, a couple of things happened.

For one thing, I started running into people carrying oxygen tanks. People with emphysema, a chronic lung condition caused by damage to the tissues of the lungs, often require a constant flow of oxygen. They have such a difficult time getting air into their lungs that they have to expend an incredible amount of energy on breathing—something a healthy person does without thought. In fact, it becomes difficult to do anything, even eat, because they have to focus on breathing. It's scary when you can't breathe, so they often suffer from severe anxiety. It is a tough way to live.

Another thing that occurred is that I would often see women dressed in business suits and corporate attire and think, *I would love to be that together and have a position that would afford me the opportunity to dress that nice.* Then, when the woman would light up a cigarette, my respect and admiration would diminish.

I noticed this feeling of disgust and couldn't help but think, *Heck, I smoke too. What does that say about me?*

This was not enough to make me stop smoking. I was not yet ready, but I was being primed, and something inside me was stirring. I started noticing things about smoking that disturbed me. For instance, I hated having to go to the store at any hour of the day or night to purchase cigarettes when I didn't plan well and ran out. I felt like a slave, and I didn't like it. I felt powerless, as though I had no choice; the cigarettes were in charge of me. I was addicted so I had to have cigarettes on hand at all times. I also hated the smell of my clothes and hair. My car windows were always dirty no matter how often I cleaned them. It was a dirty habit.

The final event occurred when I started nursing school. I had finally found some direction in my life and was excited to become a nurse. My vision for myself as a nurse, however, didn't fit with being a smoker. This was the final trigger that pushed me to change. It caused me to redefine myself: as a nurse it was out of integrity for me to smoke. Those two things did not go together for me. During the summer between my first and second years of nursing school, I became a nonsmoker and gave up smoking for good. I have never looked back.

There are things that occur in our lives over a period of time that awaken us to change—first to recognizing the possibility of change, then to believing that we need to change and that the change has value for us, then to wanting to change, and then, finally, to becoming willing to change—even, hopefully, determined to change.

When we are ready to change, we do it. We will go to any and all lengths to make the change in our reality. Consider your own life: what were the moments that something shifted in you, and you decided to change course and take a new path? It is this shift that we want to capture so we can identify strategies for motivating ourselves to change in other ways. You've already done it in some respect, so you can learn to apply those same strategies to other areas of your life.

A Moment of Acceptance

There is a moment in time when addicts stop fighting and hold up their arms in an act of surrender. They can no longer deny their addiction. They admit defeat and acknowledge that their life has become unmanageable. They have had enough, and they just cannot go on like this any longer.

This is called hitting bottom. Change is imminent. They give up pretending. They break through the denial, and they fold.

We've all experienced this in some form when we acknowledge our current reality and face the facts that things aren't the way we want them to be and they are no longer tolerable. They are the way they are, and we don't like the way things are.

Only when you face reality can you then make decisions and take action steps to change course.

It is very difficult for us to acknowledge reality as it is. We prefer to live in the lies or the stories we tell ourselves about how life is. We struggle and stress out and get angry about things over which we have no control. This is a trick of the mind. You have these ideas about how life should be, and you become attached to them being right, being the best ideas ever, and when reality differs from your ideas, you become angry. You cannot understand why life isn't as you think it should be. The gap between your fantasy and reality causes you pain and hardship.

Stop fighting reality! Accept things as they are and stop wishing for things to be as you think they should be. Things are as they are. If they *should* be different, they *would* be different.

Stop wishing for people to be different. Each of us is on our own path of understanding, and each of us travels along the continuum of personal development. There is no right, wrong, good, or bad. Suspend your judgment or your belief that people should be different. They are entitled to be where they are on their journey. Accept that this is just *where* they are, not *who* they are.

When you accept what *is*, you stop living in a fantasy and instead face what is in front of you. With acceptance of reality as it is, you empower yourself with choice. Then change is possible.

Motivated to Change

What, then, motivates us to act, to change course?

You want to exercise. Change jobs. Get a promotion. Move across country. Leave your spouse. Get married. Write a book. Buy a house. Get out of debt. Save for retirement.

But you don't take action. And you're not happy.

You tell yourself it is fine. But it's not fine. There is something missing from your life. You feel bad about not doing what your heart wants you to do. So inside you are being pulled apart. Your soul cries to you, but you struggle to heed the call. Notice the struggle. Notice the pain. Lift yourself out of denial. And then, as Will Rogers said, "If you find yourself in a hole, the first thing to do is to stop digging."

Willingness to change requires a big enough hole to hit bottom in . . . or a skylight.

Change can be thrust upon you—layoffs, death, illness, divorce, acts of nature, the car won't start, your boss relocates, your company gets sold . . . These sudden events cause change without choice. You either learn to cope with the change or get left behind, forever holding on to the past and being miserable about the present.

To be willing to change, something BIG has to happen within you. Change requires a lot of effort, so in order for you to do whatever it takes to make a life change, you will need to be highly motivated. One of two things has to happen:

1. Either you are in so much pain you can't take it anymore, or
2. You have a dream so incredible that you will do anything to achieve it.

You will move away from pain or toward pleasure. That's it. We are going to use this to our advantage.

Move away from pain

This means you become sick and tired of being sick and tired, and you become willing to experience something else. The pain has become so great that you cannot take it anymore; you cannot deny it anymore. Your life has become unmanageable, and you've had enough.

People with addictions who find their way into recovery know this all too well. Their life is in shambles, they are one step away from jail or death, and they come crawling for help. There is no other choice left but to ask for help.

This is also true of many bad relationships and toxic jobs. You wait until you can no longer justify the pain, you have no more excuses, or you simply awaken to your reality. You can no longer live in denial, and you are faced with the truth of your life.

Perhaps what triggers it for you is a heart attack, a diagnosis of pre-diabetes, or the untimely death of someone close.

Denial is what often keeps you in the hole until you have no choice but to begin your climb. Denial is just another disguise for fear. You fear the truth. You fear what will happen if you change your life.

Only when the pain is great enough will you commit to doing whatever it takes to follow through.

You've been in this place before. Perhaps you returned to college and got the grades you needed to graduate because you wanted to give yourself more opportunities to earn a living. Maybe you gave up smoking or drugs because your health was deteriorating, or you left that job because you were tired of being undervalued and mistreated.

Something shifted, and you became fed up with life as it was, and you embarked upon a new direction.

For my father, it happened one day while working as a radiologist in a hospital. He had to explain to a patient a procedure he was to perform later that day. The patient had lung cancer, so my dad asked him if he was a smoker, and the patient replied, "Not anymore!"

"When did you quit?" my dad asked.

"Two days ago, when I got the diagnosis," the man replied.

Then, my father went down to the cardiac rehab area to meet a friend—a cardiologist—for lunch. While my dad was waiting, he noticed people running on the treadmills. They all were graduates of the "Zipper Club," people who had had coronary bypass surgery (the scar down their chest looks like a zipper). Here they were, running and working out to try to get healthy and fit and decrease their stress *after* they had surgery and were spared from death (for now). They had no choice but to work out and eat right—if they wanted to live, that is.

My father wondered, *Why do we wait until something bad happens in order to make necessary changes in the way we live? Why can't we do the right thing before we get sick?*

Good question, Dad!

This was the impetus he needed to change his dietary habits and take better care of himself. Although relatively healthy, he had grown up in the days when meat and potatoes piled with butter were the main foods. He decided to change how he ate.

This is an excellent example of "pulling the bottom up." In other words, you don't need to wait until you have lung cancer to quit smoking, or your spouse hits you again to move on, or your new boss insults you again to go to human resources (or find a new job!). There is no reason to wait until the pain in your life becomes so great you cannot take it anymore. You can learn to be proactive—to care about you—and take the necessary steps to freedom by empowering yourself to create change rather than being in fear of it. Give yourself permission to go after excellence and stop putting up with stuff that makes you unhappy.

Move toward pleasure

The other way you willingly change is to envision a life that is so much better, so exciting, so wonderful that you will do absolutely anything to get there.

Consider a time in your life when you were able to make a change because you envisioned something better for yourself and your life. You wanted a new career or a particular degree or grade in school. It was important to you.

A compelling vision is very motivating.

This is generally harder to do. You may not know what you want, but you always know what you *don't* want. If you are accustomed to mediocrity, drama, busyness, or problems, then happiness and peace are not things you can easily relate to. You may not know "amazing" or "joy" or "incredible," so it is difficult to imagine life being so wonderful or easy.

It is a challenge to envision a new reality without thinking of it as a pipe dream, something so unrealistic that it's not worth wasting time dreaming about. You dream it but then write it off as not possible before your dream has time to take root. You have not yet cultivated the necessary belief in your dream for it to become viable.

Vision is essential for change to be worthwhile. Yes, you can give up what isn't working in your life. That, in fact, is a great place to begin. This will create the space for something new. Then you can decide what you want and begin to add it to your life. To sustain the change, you must want what you are creating. Moving away from pain is limiting; you will eventually run out of motivation as the pain lessens. Pursuing the pleasure you foresee in your vision will be your incentive for continuing the journey.

It takes practice. Dreams do come true, and change is possible.

The Person You Were Then

Your life is a reflection of what you value and the choices you have made up to today. To embrace change, you must let go of who you were.

Your life is like a journey of a thousand miles. Perhaps today you are strolling mile 389. Whatever happened in previous miles are stories of where you have been and the road you have traveled.

If you want to change your path, you will need to let go of your past and how you feel about it. Do not judge yourself for where you are today now that you feel the need to change course. The choices you made and the path you traveled have brought you to this point. You have grown and learned many things that you might not have done had you made different choices.

People can be very tough on themselves about the choices they made in the past. You did the best you knew how, given the person you were then and the information you had at the time. You cannot stand in this moment with the knowledge you have today and judge the person you were then as making wrong or bad choices. That's not fair.

If you had known better, you would have done better.

Today, you will do better. You will *be* better.

Forgive yourself if you must and know that nothing in life is a mistake—mistakes bring your attention to things you did not know you needed to learn. Mistakes are opportunities to grow and learn and stretch. The very things you think are mistakes are often exactly the right thing for teaching you the lesson you need in order to achieve greater and better things. Nothing is a mistake; always look for the lesson.

The person you were then is not the person you are today nor is it the person you will be as you embrace change. You will write a new story, and you will identify new values and guiding principles so that your path will take a new course into the future you envision. You will be born again.

Who you were yesterday is not who you are now. Give up who you were.

Give Up Your Story

There is a story you tell about why things are the way they are. This is the story you live by. It is what you tell yourself over and over again and have been repeating for years. This is the story you created, the explanation for your life, for why you are the way you are and for why you are *where* you are.

It's not truth. It's all in your head. It's just a story.

Stories are very powerful. The more you repeat the story, the more it becomes truth for you. What you think about you bring about. The more you accept it as truth, the more attached to the story you become. "This is who I am," you declare.

But it's not who you are; it is a story that explains where you have been, the present reality you have created, and what happened to you along the way. Your story represents your past. In fact, all stories are about the past. If you are telling the story, it already happened.

You are not your stories.

Thousands of thoughts go through your mind on any given day. Often the ones that speak the loudest are the ones you listen to; they are not necessarily your best thoughts. Your story limits you by keeping you stuck in the past. As you repeat the story over and over again, you recreate that reality in the present.

We all have stories. Lots of stories.

The first step toward change is to identify the stories you live by so you can write a new story. In order to become someone new, learn to recognize the story and stop living it. Create a new story of your future self or situation—what do you want your future to be like, look like, or feel like? This will then motivate you to create your new life, empowering you to take action toward your goals, and with each action you take, you will feel more confident, which increases your belief in the possibility for success.

Observe yourself. Pay attention to your stories and how you explain yourself and your challenges. Stories are excuses—plain and simple. Become aware of where and how you tell your stories. Notice them and notice how the story impacts your life. Is it limiting you and your happiness or success in some way? How? What are you missing because you are too attached to your story?

Let Go of Your Past

Preparing for change means letting go of your past. It means forgiving people for how they treated you, your parents for the way they behaved, and yourself for the choices you made.

Getting ready for something new means coming to terms with the way things were and recognizing—embracing—your future.

Forgiveness begins with acceptance:

- Accept that you cannot change the past—it was what it was. You can, however, change how you feel about the past, how you tell the story of your past, and what that situation or event means to you today (or what you want it to mean for you moving forward in your life).

- Accept that people are doing the best they know how, even when they do bad things. Behaviors speak volumes about where that person is on their own personal development path. It does not excuse their behavior; it merely enables you to have compassion. They may not have self-awareness or know how their behaviors impact others. Acceptance does not mean agreement. It simply means to look at reality for what it is rather than what you wish it could be, what it could have been, or what it should be. It is what it is.

- Accept that your interpretation of events, people, and situations can be flawed. Perceptions may have been skewed or misunderstood. People also remember things differently. What is the story you are telling yourself? What is it that you are holding on to? Perhaps it would be healthier to let it go and heal.

- Accept that you didn't know any better with choices you made when you were younger, even if you do know now. If you had known better then, you would have behaved differently.

Acceptance brings you out of denial. Forgiveness is then possible once you accept and are willing to acknowledge what happened to you or what you went through. Forgiveness means acknowledging your own humanity and vulnerability, and the humanity of others. Once you realize your own humanity, you can grant that to other people as well.

People do what they do—including you—because they do not know any better. That does not mean they should not be held accountable—quite the contrary. That is how we learn and grow.

However, remaining angry hurts you—both physically and emotionally. It keeps people at a distance as you maintain a wall separating you from others and keeps love from entering your heart.

Forgive because you can afford to, because you have grown beyond the hurt and pain, because there is something better to live for. Get therapeutic help if you need to and be willing to work through your pain. Do the emotional work. It is the only path to healing.

By holding on to your past, you carry baggage into the present, which has a great impact on you, your enjoyment of life, and your relationships. You make life difficult when you carry your heavy load.

Along your journey of a thousand miles, struggle and stress and pain occur. You carry these burdens with you into the next mile and the next . . . Your burden is so heavy. Perhaps it causes you physical pain. But you may not connect the two.

There you are traveling your miles carrying this burden and looking behind you, keeping track of where you've been.

You lose the present when you hold on to your past.

You also maintain your anger and hurt feelings, keeping them safely with you and ruining your present, ensuring your future is just as painful as your past.

Anger is always about the past and what has happened. It is not about the future or what *is*; it's about what *was*.

When you are angry and hateful and in pain and holding on to the past, you are not open to receiving anything new. Picture your fists closed, holding on tightly to something. How can life hand you something else if you're not open and available to receive it? You must let go and keep your hands open to allow for something new to enter.

Letting go of your past is one of the most liberating experiences. In the moment of acceptance, you move beyond the pain of your upbringing or divorce or toxic work experience. You no longer carry your burdens into the present; you give yourself the gift of freedom from your past and the energy to look toward your future.

You are now able to enjoy the present. If you cannot live in the present, you will not be able to experience joy and happiness; they do not live in the past or the future—they can only be experienced in this moment.

Being prepared for change means letting go of what came before. You will become a new person as you take on this change. The past has helped you get to this point in time; it won't help get you where you are going. Let go of trying to stay the same and be willing to become someone new—someone better. Where you are going, there is no room for the old wounds, pain, or anger. Leave the past in the past.

Begin a New Life Today

> *"Today, I begin a new life. Today I shed my old skin which hath too long suffered the bruises of failure and the wounds of mediocrity. Today I am born anew, and my birthplace is vineyard for all."*

> —*Og Mandino*

This quote from Og Mandino's perennial best seller, *The Greatest Salesman in the World*, speaks to the end of what was and the beginning of what's to come. It speaks to starting over, starting anew.

Being ready for change requires you to let go of what was, giving yourself time to heal and permission to forgive. It means embracing and honoring all that has come before in your life to bring you to this amazing place. Be grateful for all that you have been able to accomplish in your life thus far. You are a remarkable human being!

Being ready for change means that you are willing to acknowledge the emotions you experience along the way. Some days you'll feel like you cannot continue along your journey, and you may consider turning back. Other days, nothing will be able to stop you! You'll be a formidable, driving force of change.

Use the eight powerful strategies you are about to learn to help you navigate the stormy waters of change.

Today, tell yourself a new story about who you are and where you are going.

Today, make a decision to change; proclaim that you no longer want to travel the path you've been on and opt for a new direction. It's new. It's scary. But you can do it. You are a master of change!

*   *   *

Before you learn the eight simple strategies for making a change, let's first learn about what makes change hard. We begin by learning about the mind and how habits are formed.

CHAPTER 3

RELEASE THE GRIP OF OLD HABITS

---

*"Habit is a cable; we weave a thread of it each day, and
at last we cannot break it."*

—Horace Mann

A Habit Is Born

The mind is a wonderful tool. When you first learn how to do
something, anything—fold clothes, drive a car, work on a computer program, take a shower—you have to focus all your energy on
learning the steps to complete the task. With repetition and time, however, it becomes a habit where you no longer have to consciously think
about the steps to accomplishing the task; you do it without thinking.

In other words, initially, you use your conscious mind to think
about what you are doing. After performing the task enough times,
you develop neurological connections, or pathways, which then enable
your subconscious mind to function independently without your conscious awareness. It's as if you have given your subconscious permission
to take over for you because you've completed the task successfully for
so long consciously. This enables you to operate automatically.

39

The brain sets up this mechanism so that the conscious mind can focus attention on other tasks. The conscious mind can only hold one thought or feeling at a time. You might think this is not very efficient; however, the brain would differ. What this means is that the brain relies on habits so that your conscious mind can focus your attention on something new or something that requires its full attention.

This is also how it works when developing beliefs and ideas about life. Negative or positive, these thoughts—beliefs—guide your behavior behind the scenes, often without your awareness, creating a kind of operating system.

When you are young, you listen to the comments made by your parents, teachers, and family members. You listen intently to their words and the emotions behind the words. You learn through observation. You see how women treat men and how men treat women. You learn about love and relationships. You learn to feel valued—or not. You learn how emotions are handled. You learn to yell and scream—or to be silent when something bothers you. You learn to communicate respectfully and treat others with loving-kindness—or not. You learn about money—to spend or save, to treat money respectfully or to disdain it.

Most importantly, you learn how to feel about yourself. One client who had gained an inordinate amount of weight over the years said that her brothers called her chubby while they were growing up. She was put down and verbally bashed. Although they claimed they were only toying with her, the impact was great. She spent her life living up to the self-image that she was heavy and that this was all she could ever be.

This is where our beliefs and our perceptions about life, ourselves, other people—everything—come from.

The system itself is very efficient for us humans. These habits of thought and behavior become our internal guidance system enabling us to function by using the beliefs and values we have set up for ourselves as habits. They guide us behind the scenes without having to evaluate every little thing like we did when we were young and learning things for the first time. Without these habits, it would be very time consuming to accomplish anything.

This mechanism allows us to behave efficiently and to "walk and chew gum at the same time." In other words, this is how we are able to multitask. While performing one task out of habit without conscious thought, your conscious mind focuses attention on another task. Consider when you are singing in the shower. Your mind is trying to remember the words, perhaps to sing on key, but you are not consciously thinking about how to wash your body. That's a habit you developed long ago, and you follow it faithfully.

The other way people multitask is not as efficient. This is when you actually shift your attention very quickly between two or more things, like typing an email while talking on the phone. It is not possible to pay attention to both things at the same time (although many people may disagree, believing they are very efficient at this. But consider, how much of the conversation do you remember when your attention is split with typing that email?) There are some things that require your full attention and presence of mind while other things can be performed by habit. Communication and relationships always require your full attention.

Do you remember when you learned how to drive? Let's go back now to that time in your life. It was challenging, but you were so excited that you didn't really give it much thought; you were determined. You had to constantly think about where to put your feet and your hands and where to look and what to look for . . . it required your complete, unwavering attention. But then, after a few months, it became quite natural and easy, and today, you don't even think about any of that. Your body has learned how to perform the tasks of driving so well you do not need to be conscious for driving, only for navigating where you are going.

Have you ever driven home and thought, *How did I get here?*, not remembering the drive? Scary thought, eh? You were operating on autopilot, which means your attention was elsewhere. Not a good thing when driving because things can happen so fast; however, on that drive home when your conscious mind had checked out, nothing out of the ordinary occurred. Had something happened, such as an animal crossing the road or a car running a red light, you would have snapped to attention. Your mind would have been clear and alert, and you would have been attentive and engaged to manage the situation.

We spend too much of our time in this mindlessness, doing one thing while our conscious mind is somewhere else. We aren't really present for any of it, and our days float by. Awareness, or mindfulness, is crucial to being in control and in charge of our choices. Being mindful, especially when getting behind the wheel of a car with people's lives in your hands, ensures that you are in control—awake, alert, and aware.

In order to create a habit, you have to think a thought that triggers an emotional response, and then react in a certain way. This path is repeated numerous times—every time you drive your vehicle, you reinforce the thought, emotion, and action required to perform the skills.

Think about it as having a cup of T.E.A.: Thought, emotion, action. Thought, emotion, action.

All the while, your brain is creating those neurological connections to ensure this same sequence of events occurs every time you get behind the wheel of a car.

Consider this example. You want to walk to the store from your home, but there is no path through the wooded area. So you decide to create a path and find some low brush that can easily be moved aside. You walk this path regularly. Eventually, a footpath is created, and other people enjoy the shortcut. Perhaps the township decides to create a roadway through this area. This is likened to the way neurological pathways are created. They grow stronger with use and time as they are reinforced with your behaviors.

Thousands of neurological pathways are formed in order to create a habit. When you want to change a behavior pattern—drive a different route home, be more assertive, delegate more rather than do everything yourself—you have to stop before the old sequence of neurological connections is triggered and then create new connections to form new habits. This requires a tremendous amount of consistency and attention over a period of time, which is why adopting new habits is challenging. When you decide to change, suddenly everything you were doing automatically has to be scrutinized to determine whether the behavior will fit in the new landscape and will bring about the result you seek.

There are also beliefs that accompany those behaviors. You will always do what you perceive is of the greatest value to you. These are your attachments. Beliefs are like the glue that keeps you doing things over and over again the same way to ensure the neurological connections remain intact.

It is possible to create new neurological connections and habits of behavior to produce new results. In other words, you *can* teach an old dog a new trick.

New results require new thinking and new behaviors.

It Begins with a Thought

Every day, thousands of thoughts run through your mind. Scientists estimate this number to be upward of fifty thousand thoughts. That's a lot of noise! Most of these thoughts are not new to you; they are the same thoughts you have had over and over again, day after day, year after year. As mentioned before, this becomes the operating system that guides your behavior and creates your reality.

The beliefs and guiding values in your operating system may have been developed when you were very young without your informed consent. You did not consciously choose every belief or action you perform automatically. You adopted beliefs and perspectives from other people who influenced your life during your youth. Then, you became a slave to your habits.

Think about it: of the fifty thousand thoughts you have in a day, how many of those are positive and healthy thoughts? How many are critical and judgmental thoughts, telling you negative things about yourself, other people, and life? How many of these thoughts are demeaning or demanding? How many are positive, kind, and supportive?

You become what you think about all day long.

If these habits are good, then you like them. You can trust them, and you want to keep them. If you think, for example, that you bounce back from setbacks easily, then you will find a way to handle adversity when presented with something unpleasant. But if your habits of mind and behavior are not bringing you the results you want, then they require revisiting for updating and correcting. Consider, for example, that you don't speak up in meetings because you do not think that what you have to say is important or that anyone will want to hear it. This thinking does not serve you and may be rooted in beliefs you have about yourself. It may be holding you back from being promoted or from other achievements since no one hears your ideas.

Some habits are consciously created, such as driving. But most of the habits you create, you don't pay much attention to. The beliefs you formed about yourself and what is possible for you in your life, for instance, you most likely did not consciously create.

In order to change, you will need to assess the habits of thought that govern your actions and choose new thoughts to form new habits.

If this sounds hard, well, it is. Habits cannot be broken; they have to be replaced with new habits, and that requires work. This is why they are a barrier to success. It is also why we will take a different approach to dealing with habits as we embark upon learning to make change easier.

CHAPTER 4

LET GO OF ATTACHMENTS

"The tighter you squeeze, the less you have."

—Zen Saying

This Too Shall Pass

Life is filled with change, and all things are temporary. What lives will die. Seasons come and seasons go. All of life is change.

It is our desire for things to be as we want them to be that causes us angst and pain. This is our suffering. We cling to what we have. We chase what we think we want, and we get caught up in this charade when, in fact, what we really want, what we long for, and what we really need is peace, happiness, joy, respect, fulfillment, love, health, and freedom.

However, instead of looking within to discover and experience these things, we look outside ourselves and become attached to things we *think* will make us happy. We chase after possessions, people, money, status, fame, and fortune looking for a sense of stability in ourselves. But we are left empty because we will never find ourselves in any of those things.

We can also become attached to our beliefs and ideas about life, ourselves, and other people. When our ideas of reality (our fantasies) differ from actual reality, we suffer. We become frustrated and angry. Things are not as we think they should be, and this is a source of stress.

The things you create in your mind are illusions, possibilities, perspectives; they are not real. They are mental creations, constructions created with your imagination. The mind is a wonderful playground!

Identifying your attachments, fears, worries, and pain will help you to let go and move on so you can create the change you want.

Acceptance is the key to opening the door. It is where your power lies. Right now, your attachments hold the power. The ideas in your mind that you hold tightly keep you unhappy and stuck. These are attachments. It is time to let go so you can invite new people, new ideas, new things, and new experiences into your life.

All things will end—good and bad. You mustn't cling to any of it. Enjoy the experiences life presents you—desirable and undesirable. In truth, it just *is*. We label things as "good" or "bad" because we judge. We either like what we get, or we don't. But in reality, it is what it is— neither good nor bad.

Addicted to Your Thoughts

When you are contemplating something, you have ideas. Lots of ideas. Your mind sorts through these ideas and plays with them, shapes them, until, at last, you have come up with the perfect idea, solution, or point of view. You've solved the problem. You have the answer.

This is a function of the mind. It is wonderful how it toys with ideas. This is not a problem. It's fun!

The problem is that people can become very attached to their ideas being the best ideas. After all, you have the perfect idea. And if your idea is perfect, then it is *right*, which would mean anyone else's idea is *wrong*.

We can put up quite a fight in order to get our *right* ideas heard and taken seriously. This can result in arguments, competition, even war, and a win-lose mentality. We yell and scream to get our ideas heard. We force our ideas onto others because "Can't you see how right I am!" And, in so doing, we may not be so nice in the process. Actually, we can be quite nasty.

In these moments, we are valuing our ideas over everything else. The idea, this perfect idea, we treat as being more important and special than the human being standing in front of us. We elevate this idea to having greater value than even our dignity. Think about it, yelling at the top of your lungs is never graceful and dignified. Neither is cursing, rolling your eyes at someone, or making faces.

People do not realize that this is what happens when they are arguing with their spouse or their boss or their kids. When you are gripped by this thought process, it's as if your compassion valve is shut off and there is no way in. You have put up a wall behind which your true self is hiding, and this thought process is now in command.

Gripped by this idea that you are right, and the rest of the world is wrong, your threat level rises, and, mentally, you prepare to fight! Your stress level increases as this becomes emotional for you, and these emotions mean that, in this moment, another part of your brain is at work. Your conscious mind can only hold on to one thought or feeling at a time. If you are emotional, then you are not able to process ideas rationally. Your emotional mind, the limbic center, is functioning, and your frontal cortex, where mental processing takes place, is shut off.

In other words, you cannot think and feel at the same time.

You might as well stop, breathe, and have your discussion when you are calm. That way, you avoid having to do damage control later with this wonderful human being with whom you are speaking.

Ideas are never more important than people. Yet, in our minds, given the right circumstances, we can believe so greatly in our ideas that nothing else seems to matter as much.

We must break ourselves free from this perspective and elevate the human being to its rightful spot in the hierarchy of value. People are always more important than thoughts and ideas.

Being attached to your ideas, thoughts, and beliefs is a huge barrier to change because when you believe you are right and everyone else is wrong, well, how can you possibly learn new things? How can you begin to create new beliefs about your life and your future if you are attached to your old thoughts being true, perfect, and right?

Welcome to Your Wall

"We have met the enemy and he is us."

—*Pogo (comic strip)*

In his work on value science and axiology, Robert Hartman, PhD, quantified the concept of "value," which is the valuing of all things in the universe from infinitely positive to infinitely negative. The hierarchy of value explains that there is a natural law or order of how things are valued in the universe. In essence, he identified that the greater the number of properties something has, the greater the value. In short, a human life, a singular concept unable to be identically duplicated in any form, is of greatest value, along with other spiritual elements. The second level of value includes inanimate objects such as a chair or a car. And the third level of value includes intangibles such as ideas, thoughts, or concepts.

What this means is that people come first. When you are yelling or arguing with another human being—a boss, spouse, or customer—you are valuing something else over that human being: your ideas, being right, or being heard.

The most important characteristic to display in dealing with people is empathy. Only through empathy can you seek to understand that person, their perspective, and what they really want or need in that moment.

Consider how a person responds to you when you go to them to discuss a problem or frustration. All too often, the person responds (they may even interrupt before you have completed sharing your situation) by telling you what to do, sharing their story of a similar frustrating situation, or trying to fix the problem for you. How does this make you feel when this happens? Do you feel heard, supported, validated? Or do you feel dismissed and diminished?

Imagine instead the person listens until you are finished speaking, asks some questions to ensure they have understood what the real problem is for you, questions you about the challenge you are having with this problem, and then helps you determine what options you may have available to solving it. How might that feel different?

It takes quite a bit of personal development to move beyond our own personal needs to be able to empathize and be with that human being rather than seek to have your own needs met, be right, have the answer, or turn the conversation around so the focus is on you. It requires a high level of self-awareness and self-mastery to be able to listen to, be curious about, and value the person rather than try to fix or problem-solve for that person.

When someone empathizes with us, they ask questions nonjudgmentally and are genuinely curious about us and what we are thinking, feeling, and experiencing. We begin to feel safe, validated, and valued as a capable and competent human being, which helps to bring down the wall that separates us from others.

Dr. Hartman identified that people hold back a significant portion of their productivity and cooperation behind a wall of resistance or fear. This wall is comprised of old wounds, fears, attitudes, beliefs, history, trauma, and pain. The wall goes up quite quickly in response to judgment, but when a person feels that they are cared about and valued as a human being, without judgment, then they feel as though it is okay to simply be themselves and stop pretending. They feel safe enough to bring down their wall, be vulnerable, and let you in a bit. It is only then that we can truly connect with each other.

If the wall remains, then we will only connect with their wall, not the incredible person that hides behind it.

We all have walls. Whenever we interact, there is an opportunity to bring down the walls that separate us. Or we can go about our life with our own agenda, not caring about the fragile nature of human life, and stomp all over each other in a myriad of ways. When we argue, for instance, what really happens is that both of our walls are bumping up against each other while our true selves cower behind our respective walls of protection.

We hide behind our walls because we do not feel safe to come out and play. We feel the need to pretend; we have not yet learned to feel comfortable being our wonderful selves without the wall to hide behind. And the individual did not create the safety needed for you to emerge from behind your wall of protection.

Learning to love, honor, and respect yourself will help you to bring down your wall so you can free yourself and unleash your potential. Empathy helps you create the safe space for others to do the same.

The Value of You

Somewhere in your thought processes, you have ideas and beliefs about yourself and where you rank in the scheme of things. As a human being, you are irreplaceable, unique, and priceless. As such, you are of greatest value. Interestingly, you may not have difficulty believing in the infinite and priceless value of a human being. You are quite capable of recognizing this value in others. The difficulty may be in embracing *your* value, in acknowledging and accepting that you, too, are a human being and fit into the same category as everyone else.

Most of the population experiences self-doubt. To the degree that you are comfortable with yourself, this doubt may not interfere with your daily life. But for many people, it gets in the way of experiencing true happiness and close relationships. It becomes part of the wall that they erect between themselves and others, questioning who they are and what they do so often that they become preoccupied with themselves. They are so busy questioning and doubting themselves, trying to impress and pretend for others (hoping no one finds out the horrible things they think about themselves) that there is not a lot of space for other people.

When you don't believe that you are of great value as a human being, you will look for your value elsewhere. This is reflected in your self-esteem as it attempts to overcompensate for feelings of "not good enough" or "less than." The "self" has to have value, you see. So if you are not giving it to yourself, you will go elsewhere to find it.

The problem with this plan of action is that you are always searching and never quite receiving what you need in order to feel good about yourself. You are dependent upon others to value you appropriately in the hopes of getting what you've always been able to (and can only) give to yourself.

You might seek validation or value through your ideas and opinions, often finding yourself defensive, in battle with others to defend your ideas and to defend yourself. Defensiveness is a clear sign that your self-worth is tied to your ideas.

You might look for value in your work, accomplishments, possessions, or relationships. You might focus on impressing others with the right clothes or car or lifestyle or spouse. In your quest to find your value, you might accomplish great things, but that feeling of completeness continues to elude you, or you experience only short-lived satisfaction.

All these little games you play leave you vulnerable because when you look for value in something outside you, you give up your control and your power. Your power lies in valuing yourself and enjoying the incredible human being you are. Your power lies in choosing healthy thoughts and actions.

People who enjoy high self-esteem get their self-worth from how highly they value human life and the understanding that they, too, are human. These people get it—they get that they are amazing because they are human. They understand the value of their own humanity and feel comfortable being themselves without any need to impress or hide themselves. This frees them to simply be who they are. It's very liberating.

Often, people who have achieved a level of success in recovery from addiction learn this lesson and reach a high level of self-esteem. They learn through the process of recovery that life is of greatest value. Remember, they come from a place where they didn't believe their life was worth anything. They were hiding from themselves and suppressing their pain. Over time as they face their fears, adopt new stories, and accept themselves, they come to understand that just the opposite is true: there is nothing of greater value than a human life, and the most important one for them to care for is their own. They learn, finally, to love and value themselves and the gift of life.

People with high self-esteem demonstrate confidence and display a feeling of self-assuredness. They are comfortable with themselves and don't worry about proving themselves to others. Instead, they are simply true to themselves. They honor themselves. In so doing, they are free to empathize and to help others. They are also free to enjoy themselves because they spend less time trying to impress or please others or being concerned about what other people think of them. They simply are who they are.

Being caught up in your own chase for self-worth is time-consuming. You have little mental space to deal with other people. It interferes with your ability to communicate effectively and to develop relationships that are enjoyable and natural.

Imagine for a moment that your self-worth is attached to your ideas. You share an idea at a meeting. Someone says they have a different idea. How does that feel? Do you feel crushed, like someone just kicked you in the gut? Since they had a new idea that differs from your own, your mind, craving its daily dose of self-worth, interprets the rejection of your idea to mean "They don't like *me*." Wow. So you fight for your idea because you cannot allow your "self" to have no value (even though it's just an idea).

In this dynamic, are you listening to the other people in the room, or are you more focused on being heard, being right, or being recognized for this great idea? Consider the other people in the room: If many of them also link their self-worth to their thoughts and ideas, how well are they listening and how defensive do they become when their ideas are passed over? People in these situations don't feel valued or validated. They don't feel heard, and too much time is spent on defensiveness without truly listening or trying to understand one another. The original problem gets lost in the pandemonium of self-serving affirmation.

When your self-worth is attached to your ideas and you are speaking with someone who is pushing their ideas on you or who is not really listening to you because they are attached to their own ideas, your self-esteem is threatened. When they push their ideas on you, they act as though they are right, and they seem to be making you wrong. What you hear is not that *your idea has no merit*, but rather *you have no merit. You* are wrong.

That's not what they mean; what they mean is that they are attached to their idea, and they don't like your idea, or they may not have even heard your idea because they were so attached to sharing their own idea!

But when your self-worth is attached to your ideas, what you hear is that they don't like *you*, that *you* are wrong. *You* don't matter. And you are hurt. Your self-esteem has to fight for its value because it gets its value from your ideas, and you become defensive. You put up your dukes and prepare to fight.

You fight for your right to exist and to have value. At this point, your ideas—yours or the other person's—don't matter. You are hurt, and the relationship is damaged. There is now tension in the air that will need to be relieved or else fester between you.

You are so much more than your ideas.

Create Space

"Anything you cannot relinquish when it has outlived its usefulness possesses you. And in this material age, a great many of us are possessed by our possessions."

—*Mildred Lisette Norman*

We can be attached to all sorts of things, including items, ideas, people, routines, habits, being right, having control . . . It is essential to identify your attachments in order to break free from them and create the change you want.

Your attachments keep you stuck. They will not help you to move forward.

My neighbor doesn't throw much of anything away, except his empty beer bottles. He has little space in his life for anything or anyone. He chooses to live this way.

A woman shared that she longed for a companion, but she, too, had loads of stuff from years of hoarding. She had difficulty letting anything go. Every item had some sentimental value (or excuse) assigned to it. But she knew that if she wanted a relationship and friends, if she wanted to entertain and have people over, she had to create space— both physical space and mental space. There was clutter in her home and also clutter in her mind!

People can become very attached to their stuff! Material objects that no longer bring you joy or comfort and are no longer of use are attachments. Stop making excuses and get rid of them!

"Stuff" is easy because you can see the items and the boxes. You can touch them. Perhaps you even pay for the storage of all your stuff that you don't use. The storage industry has become a multi-billion-dollar industry since 1960 when it began. That is good money you could be saving for retirement or using for a vacation each year.

"Stuff" carries energy and takes up space. When you hold on to stuff, you are not open to receive. Your space is too cluttered. By de-cluttering your space physically, mentally, and emotionally, you shift your energy and create the space needed for new things to show up.

Emotions Are Messages

How do you know when you're attached to something? Emotions show you the way.

You take the same route home every day. It's short and direct. One day, a construction crew detours you off the main road. They will be working on the road for three months. How angry do you become? Do you easily accept the situation and shift to the new traffic pattern? Or are you more likely to curse and swear, complain to anyone who will listen, and maintain that anger throughout the three months as you travel the extra mile out of your way every day both to and from work?

Your spouse breaks a dish. A coworker walks off with your pen. You cannot find your favorite sweater. How angry are you?

Emotions are like little informational messages telling you something. If something makes you happy, then that tells you this is good. If something triggers anger, then there has been a transgression, and there is something you need to acknowledge, understand, and perhaps deal with. Each emotion has its own message to share and requires your assessment.

Identifying the emotion is the first step, then you take action to acknowledge it and respond to the message it has sent you.

Emotions inform you of what you are holding on to. Anger and sadness are part of the mourning process. You will experience these emotions as you travel the path toward acceptance.

Fear shows up as anxiety, panic, or worry. It often causes you to freeze rather than do anything. The message fear brings is one of danger. It can be a real danger, such as when you are about to be attacked, or it can be the false fear, when you stretch beyond the limits of your comfort zone.

Anxiety, panic, frustration, jealousy, sadness, happiness, and joy all bring you different messages. When you understand the message, you can then choose actions appropriate for bringing things back into balance.

Emotions are energy in motion. Most people don't manage their emotions well. They don't know how, so they become scared. As a society, we don't teach people how to master their emotional world. We try to understand what we feel but are often told we shouldn't feel those feelings. Then we think we are wrong for feeling what we feel. We may even feel ashamed for feeling a certain way. We rationalize our emotions and question our interpretation of the situation, perhaps even blaming ourselves. We don't trust our emotions or our explanation for them, so we contain the emotion in an imaginary box and store it somewhere in our body or mind until one day, there is no more room, and we explode. The explosion can take place as a literal one where there is yelling and screaming. It can also take the form of a physical manifestation of disease. The anger has "eaten away" at you, and now you have high blood pressure or an ulcer; or your fear and worry have caused the inflammation in your bowels. Emotions are also a reason we overeat, leading to obesity and the associated health problems.

Emotion often triggers a behavioral reaction as opposed to a controlled or conscious response. The emotion hits you, and before you have a chance to understand the message and think it through, you react. This reaction is habit: an ingrained neurochemical response that leads to an automatic behavioral reaction.

Awareness of your emotions will help you embrace your personal power by giving you choice so you can take charge. When you experience an emotion, pause. Give yourself a "time out" to assess the emotion. What are you feeling? What information is this emotion providing? And then, how would you like to respond to the situation?

Attachment can show up as stubbornness. The tighter the grip of the attachment, the stronger the emotional reaction you will experience. You hold on tight and insist on something being a certain way. You may even behave like a two-year-old, stomping your feet and wishing things would stay the same or demanding people listen to you. That's a sign that you are attached to your own thinking. It's never pretty. You will argue and defend your ideas. You will not be interested or open to hearing other people's opinions or points of view.

Look for places where your stubbornness shows up. This brings your attention to ideas and beliefs that you are attached to.

Letting go of attachments is freeing. Notice areas of struggle and consciously choose to give up the struggle, let go, and surrender to what is. What might you need to accept in this situation? When you are able to see the situation for what it is and not what you want it to be, you realize that holding on had no merit; it added no value. The act of holding on was habit.

The goal of letting go of attachments is so you can be open to new concepts and be free from the ideas and habits that bind you and hold you back. By letting go, you are able to explore new possibilities, new ideas, and new worlds! Who knows what you'll find. You may discover that a habit of yours is good and that certain ways of thinking, believing, or behaving are good for you. Letting go of attachments simply means that you are flexible and adaptable and open to choosing your response rather than to being at the mercy of your habit or emotional reactions.

CHAPTER 5

FACE YOUR RESISTANCE

---

*"I quit being afraid when my first venture failed, and
the sky didn't fall down."*

—Allen H. Neuharth

Meet Your Greatest Enemy

Habits are hard to deal with. They require time, attention, and consistency to create new ones, which is why we must find a way around tackling bad habits head-on. Attachments are hard and cause stress and struggle. You have become so accustomed to thinking a certain way that to unhinge yourself from your thoughts—to separate your self-worth from your thoughts and ideas—is very difficult. You are also attached to people, places, and things. You will need to detach from your routines, everything you are accustomed to. You have created a comfort zone, and these are the things you know. We become attached to what we know. Uncertainty and the unknown are scary. In order to change, we need to let go, and we need to face our fear.

There are other forces at work that interfere with your efforts to change. Resistance is one of them. Resistance holds you back from doing what you know you want or need to do for yourself. You want to change, but your resistance, which shows up as procrastination and avoidance behaviors, makes you believe that you cannot, you shouldn't, you don't really want to. It cons you into believing that you need to stay right here where you are. Resistance keeps you stuck.

Behind the resistance is fear. Fear is the real culprit. Fear is the reason you don't change. Fear is the reason you don't follow through. This fear is another trick of the mind. This fear is not real. It is a ploy to keep you safely within your comfort zone—safe, and comfortably unhappy.

Thoughts trigger fear, and your fear results in resistance. The experience then creates a wall behind which you hide, and the wall grows thicker and more comfortable over time. Your pattern of fear and resistance behaviors are habits, and they, too, will need to be exposed so you can break through and stop hiding behind the wall.

Over the years, I have identified fear and self-doubt as my greatest enemy:

- Fear of not being good enough.
- Fear of succeeding.
- Fear of what others would think.
- Fear of rejection—of being different, not being accepted, and being alone.
- Fear of the unknown, of taking the road less traveled and embarking upon a path that is different than other people take.

Fear holds me back. I resist doing what I need to do. I get in my own way. I create obstacles, succumb to distractions, make excuses, and rationalize. I create stories. My stories are very convincing. I sabotage my success. Although something might be uncomfortable and I may be unhappy, the situation is familiar, and change requires so much effort.

You have your own stories of resistance and procrastination.

I do recognize my resistance; I feel the fear. It nudges me to take heed and gather the resources I need to move through it. I surround myself with people who expect my best and tolerate nothing less. A great coach can help with this too. They challenge my excuses and expose my blind spots. With their support and accountability, I face my fears and confront the obstacles that limit my success. Below is an example of my thought process when personally dealing with fear.

> *The one thing I fear more than anything is not living to my potential, reaching the end of this lifetime with my books still in my head or half-written in my computer. I don't want to reach the end of my life feeling like there is so much more to do, more to contribute, and more to experience. It is this fear that pushes me to do more, see more, learn more, ask more questions, and be more.*

Fear rears its ugly head every time we want to change, any time we reach for a new level of success and make an attempt to leave our comfort zone. It creates an internal battle that plays out something like this:

- You are stuck in your own head, the same thoughts going back and forth, back and forth, back and forth.
- You see no alternatives.
- You get tired, so very tired.
- You just want it to stop.
- You get angry. Enraged perhaps.
- You become depressed.
- You are paralyzed.
- You withdraw into your shell.
- You explode at anyone close to you.

Your emotions take you for a ride. Fear wins, and you resist change. You can't move. You push people away. You may become depressed. Your relationships suffer. You are not motivated to do anything (except make things more miserable for yourself). You may find ways to escape.

Fear causes pain. If not tamed, it will run you over and beat you down. You feel lost, defeated, and disappointed.

And what are the results?

Things stay the same. You succumb to the status quo and beat yourself up for not changing, not acting. And then you feel completely spent, unhappy, drained, and disappointed yet again. And the voice in your head says, *See, I knew you wouldn't do it!*

This is a self-fulfilling prophecy. We create the thinking that holds us back and sabotages us. We conjure up limiting beliefs to explain why we can't, we manufacture stories to rationalize to others, and we make excuses for ourselves.

Fear does not have to win yet again! You can take charge!

You can give in to the fear, or you can choose to take action to move beyond the fear, beyond the resistance, beyond the excuses. As John Maxwell says, you can feed the fear or feed your faith.

Moving beyond your fear is essential to creating the changes you want and to living the life you love.

We are all fearful; it is a fundamental human emotion. In fact, it is at the foundation of every other emotion. It has a purpose.

Fear can warn you of danger. It can let you know that someone is not to be trusted. It can inform you that something is not safe.

Resistance, or fear, can also be a signal that you're not yet ready to proceed. This is helpful in that it stops you from going down a path when you are not yet prepared. This one is tricky and requires acute self-awareness and honesty. Resistance is sneaky, and it can mask itself as fear trying to prevent you from going into danger when, in fact, its purpose is to hold you back.

Emotions are messages providing you with information. Unfortunately, they are not specifically spelled out for you. I often wish that the "tap on the shoulder" that emotions provide would come with a sticky note listing instructions! Unfortunately, it doesn't happen that way. You have to interpret their meaning. You have to be honest with yourself, which is not always easy to do. We can resist the truth too! We may fear that the truth will hurt us more than the lie we live by. Denial can create a strong wall of resistance.

Another message fear can send is that you are on the right track, that you are touching the edge of your comfort zone and extending beyond what you have known before. If you flip over the fear, you often find excitement. It shows up in the same way as fear and is just as awesome, so we can easily mistake the message.

It is not our fear that's the problem; it is learning to manage the fear. As Susan Jeffers tells us in her book of the same title, we must learn to "feel the fear, and do it anyway."

Even the most successful people experience fear; some of us become paralyzed by it while others learn to achieve success in spite of it, and some even thrive on it.

When you are fearful, you may:

- Avoid taking necessary action, often making things worse but hoping the problem will just go away.
- Imagine catastrophes, create unnecessary drama in your life, and become totally stressed out.
- Rationalize and make excuses, adopt a victim mentality, and become a master procrastinator.
- Allow your fear to overwhelm you into submission, in which case you wind up changing nothing and continuing to put up with your pain.

Fear can paralyze and sabotage your success. It causes stress, and when it wins, fear beats down your self-esteem.

You don't want to do battle with your fear; fear is a formidable opponent. Instead, acknowledge your fear, recognize the message it brings, thank it for showing up (as you knew it would), and face it by acting in spite of the fear and thereby growing bigger than your fear. Instead of being at its mercy, use the message fear brings to take control of your life.

Fear Exposed

False fear is an emotion that occurs in response to an idea, a thought you have about whatever trigger or event occurs. It is an illusion; it's not real fear. Real fear occurs when you are facing true danger, such as a car moving into your lane from the other side of the road or a wild animal charging at you.

False fear, however, feels real because it initiates the same neurochemical response as if you were in real peril, but it is not triggered as a result of real danger. This fear is often referred to as: False Evidence Appearing Real.

If most of the thousands of thoughts you have every day are obsessive, repetitive thoughts, then each time you think a thought, it becomes familiar, and you reinforce the value of that thought in your mind. That thought seems true to you. If you also associate some meaning or feeling with that thought, this also reinforces the value of the thought.

Your thoughts then lead to a behavioral response. You have a thought and respond. Do this enough and, through a cascade of events in your brain, you learn to respond automatically. You are now programmed to behave in a certain way.

So when you consider alternatives, this threatens the system. Your normal operating system sends out a warning: *You can't do that! That's not how it's done!* and fear sets in. Adrenaline and cortisol are released into the bloodstream, and you are on alert. It feels as though danger is imminent, so you freeze. You feel the fear and stop. It doesn't feel good, so you figure, *I must not go there.*

False fear is a response to a threat in your mind, nothing more. It is not real fear warning you of real danger, although it feels real because of the chemical reaction in your body. The more you entertain your fear the bigger the fear gets and the less comfortable you feel challenging it. Every time you experience the fear, you reinforce its strength and give your power away to it.

In addition, you are in your own head! You have only your own same, familiar, repetitive thoughts in there. This is not a happy place to be!

Anticipatory Fear

Have you ever been frightened about something that already happened? Fear is not a past emotion; it occurs in the moment of a specific, current danger or an anticipated threat. Anticipatory fear relates to what is about to happen or what could happen, and it manifests in different ways:

1. Fear can be the past projected into the future:
   - *Every time we work together, there are problems.*
   - *I can never seem to make the right decisions.*
   - *I always have to walk on eggshells with that person.*
   - *I always mess up.*
   - *I am nervous about how my boss will react.*

You can imagine how this thinking will stop you in your tracks. When you have a history with someone or with a particular situation, you expect it to repeat itself. You anticipate the same scenario occurring again and again. If the first time didn't turn out well, then you expect the same thing to transpire this time too and to evoke the same emotions you felt last time.

Expectations are imaginary; they are guesses, thoughts that create a story incorporating assumptions and hopes. And, oh, how we become attached to our expectations! And when the expectations are not met, an emotional response ensues.

This is a wonderful opportunity, however, to revisit your previous experience and reevaluate it so you can move beyond it. What are you really afraid of? And is that belief or thought true?

2. Fear can also be characterized by the "what if" game played in our heads:

- *What if I don't make it?*
- *What if they laugh at me?*
- *What if I can't finish in time?*
- *What if they don't like me?*

This is an endless cascade of illusionary, negative possibilities. Once stuck in this thought process, you are apt to become overwhelmed and paralyzed.

Change may be challenging, but living in this uncomfortable space is hard!

Name Your Fear

Fear gets the better of you when it lurks in the shadows, hides in the bushes, and operates in secret. You must expose your fear! Get it out in the open so you can face it!

In order to *tame* your fear, you must *name* your fear. What are you scared of?

Here are some examples:

- Fear of rejection.
- Fear of succeeding.
- Fear of failing.
- Fear of losing everything.
- Fear of losing control or of being controlled.
- Fear of making the wrong choice (being wrong).
- Fear of being overwhelmed and not being able to follow through; fear that you took on too much.

Identify your fear. Get to know it. What are you afraid of? Some people are surprised by their fear. One client was surprised to discover that her biggest fear was that if she succeeded in her business, she would make more money than her husband and she was not sure how he would feel about that. This fear was holding her back from taking her business to the next level. She was leaving money on the table and not making the impact on society that she could be making once she faced her fear (selling her services, hiring employees as she expanded product lines, etc.).

In this case, she needed to have a conversation with her husband.

Another woman admitted that she recognized fear when she would retreat into silly games. She would stop working on her project, and her creativity would be stifled. At these moments she realized that fear of success was crippling her.

Many people fear losing control. When my leadership clients discuss their overwhelm and inability to delegate, often the fear of letting go of control is the culprit. They struggle to allow others to assume responsibility for work for fear of losing control or of being wrong. Fear of making a mistake often holds people back from making decisions.

If you don't know your fear, then it will continue to run your life behind the scenes. If you don't identify it, you will remain stuck wondering why you have not acted on your goal, why you behave in "silly" ways and avoid doing the very thing you know you want—and need—to do. This is often what brings your attention to your fear.

The problem with fear is that the more we think about it, the bigger it becomes. The more we focus on the obstacles, the bigger they become. But, with that same logic, the more you focus on what you want, the bigger *that* becomes: the more committed, the more focused, and the more successful you become.

What you think about all day long is what you create in reality.

Once you identify your fear, you can strategize how you want to handle it. Your vigilant awareness will help you recognize it when it rears its ugly head, and being aware of it empowers you to choose how you want to manage it. You can choose to give in to your fear, or you can choose to rise above your fear.

No one who has stood up to their fear has regretted it. In fact, when you spend time with or read about people who are dying, they consistently admit they wish they took more risks. They regret the time they wasted on unfounded fear and worries that never came to pass. They wish they had forgiven themselves and others more readily.

When you take charge of your fear, only then can you create a fabulous, fun, joyful life where you are at peace and confident in your power.

Struggle Equals Resistance

There is a place where you find yourself struggling, complaining, and wishing things were different. You sense that you are a square peg trying desperately to fit into a round hole. You may be stressed out, angry, and frustrated. You know this place. We've all been there.

Struggle is a clear message that you are resisting something. It occurs when you refuse to accept reality. It is like walking into a wall hoping the wall will move out of your way. You wonder why your head hurts so much, but you keep walking into the wall and bumping your head over and over again. You keep doing the same thing over and over again expecting different results.

You get angry and frustrated, but things don't change; the wall won't budge.

The moment you let go and accept your reality— "Hey, there is a wall here!"—suddenly your stress is relieved. It's as if the weight of the world is lifted off your shoulders. You can breathe easy again—or for the first time.

What are you resisting? What is it you are unwilling to face?

Change is hard when we resist it. Struggle is optional. Change can be easily embraced when we open ourselves up and surrender to what is. We have to stop fighting reality. This is another way our attachments show up. We are attached to our thoughts about the way things should be.

Denial is a strong force. It keeps us "stuck in the muck," as I call it. Our emotions offer us clues to our unhappiness. Oftentimes, if you just listen to yourself complain or explain or make excuses, you start to finally hear yourself, and you acknowledge your pain.

Become the observer of yourself, a spectator of your actions. Become aware of your resistance by paying attention to your emotions and actions—or lack of action. Where are you struggling? What do you need to accept? We spend so much time trying to move walls! We fight the system rather than accept the system as it is and then learn new ways to navigate through the system with integrity or find a new system that more closely parallels our values.

If you find yourself walking into a wall, stop hitting your head and make the choice to change course. Stop inflicting pain on yourself.

Self-Doubt and Judgment Kill Dreams

Everyone experiences self-doubt at some point in their life. For many people, however, self-doubt can be pervasive, even crippling. It can impact your relationships. It destroys confidence. It causes procrastination or lack of effort. It can be extremely frustrating to live with an echoing voice in your head telling you you're not good enough.

On your journey to change, doubts creep in. You question everything from your worthiness and deservingness to your abilities and skills. *Can I really do it? Will I be successful? Can I be successful? Is it possible for me?* The day ends with you hoping for a reprieve only to have these same thoughts repeat tomorrow and the next day and the next. You get stuck in your head. It's not a fun place to be.

It is very sad that for some reason we do this to ourselves. Much of what we say in the privacy of our minds we would never say to another human being. So what gives us the right to entertain these thoughts? You are so special, unique, and wonderful. There is nothing of greater value! And nowhere in the world, past or present, has there ever been anyone like you.

Is there something you gain by being so cruel to yourself?

There is a huge cost to both you and to society at large for these negative and self-disparaging remarks in your mind. You lose because you don't take risks, you're not as productive as you can be (all of those thoughts and constant self-assessing slow you down), and you are not happy because deep down inside you know you can do more, be more, and contribute more to the world. Your relationships are not as deep and meaningful because you hide the best of you behind your wall of self-doubt that has you questioning your desirability, your looks, your personality, your deservingness. Society loses because we don't reap the benefits from your talents and skills and abilities that you hide behind your wall of fear and doubt.

Sometimes doubt can be good when it causes us to question our direction and focus: *Can* you really pull this off? *Do* you have the ability, knowledge, and capacity to complete the task? Those are important questions and help to challenge your level of commitment.

Doubting because you lack faith in yourself won't nurture your success.

Self-doubt is grounded in fear: fear of your greatness, fear of your power, fear of success. What if you really are that brilliant and wonderful? What if you really can be wealthy, successful, a great leader, and in the relationship of your dreams? What then? Imagine the possibilities.

There is no benefit to doubting yourself and questioning your ability to the point of not pursuing your dreams. It only serves to stop you from becoming better than you are and living larger.

Judging yourself harshly adds to the resistance. It is a way to sabotage your efforts. You put yourself down and make disparaging comments about yourself. This reinforces the negative perceptions you have of yourself. This does not honor you or show you any respect. The impact keeps you stuck right where you are, even if the comments are made in your own mind.

Accepting our humanity is part of the growth and development each of us must make along the way. We all make mistakes. We've all been hurt. We have all hurt others. Learning to forgive, making amends where possible and appropriate, learning from our mistake so it does not repeat, and moving on is part of the maturing process.

Mistakes, much like emotions, are messages for you. They inform you of something you didn't know you needed to know. They offer you the opportunity to be taught something new—if you are open to the lesson.

Never put yourself down. It is a bad habit and one that you need to grow out of. Stop wasting time doubting and judging yourself harshly. It adds no value and can only cause harm.

Recognize the disparaging and negative remarks or thoughts and stop them. Apologize silently to yourself and stop making excuses for not doing what is in your best interest and for not treating yourself with the respect you deserve.

Instead, learn to lift yourself up. Spend more time looking for what is good about you. It's amazing how often we focus on the negatives and don't look for or notice the positives!

For change to take place, start giving yourself credit where credit is due. Look for what you do well.

Procrastination Is Resistance in Disguise

Sometimes, we procrastinate because we don't know where to begin. This is an excuse for not beginning. The answer is to begin where you are, to look for the resources needed to get started. Perhaps you are not yet ready to begin.

Sometimes, we procrastinate because we need time to consider our options. We are not yet committed to change, or we are scared, so we put off making a decision and taking action.

Some people procrastinate because they fear not being perfect. The fear of making a mistake is so great that they don't get started. Why bother? Or they enter into a project, but they don't finish. Their self-esteem is so entangled with being perfect that they are paralyzed by their resistance.

Perfectionism is an excuse, a story, and a habit of thought that serves only to keep you from enjoying yourself and doing your best. The concept of perfection is all in your mind. It is another game your mind plays with you to keep you from achieving the happiness and success you desire.

Procrastination is the avoidance of doing what you know you need to do. Unfortunately, it causes tremendous stress and zaps your energy. Throughout the day you have thoughts about the project you said you wanted to begin. But you don't act. So you give yourself a little beating. *You really should get started. You should do that. Why can't you just do it? You know this is good for you.* This may go on for several minutes.

Later in the day, you are reminded yet again that you have not done what you know you'd like to do. You give yourself another beating, wasting more time and disparaging yourself a little (or a lot) more. This repeats several times throughout your day—every day—for every change you've been thinking about making but are not taking action on.

Every time you don't work out, every time you raise your voice, every time you don't speak up in a meeting, every time you miss a deadline, you are reminded of your lack of action to change and give yourself a little beating.

By the end of the day, you are battered and bruised. No wonder you have no energy!

Every so often, procrastination serves a purpose. I call it "incubation time," when we put something off because we are just not yet ready to write it, sketch it, draw it, or work on it.

In this instance, however, you are making a conscious choice. You choose to procrastinate or put something off when you are not yet ready to decide. If you then schedule it in your calendar for a later time, this is not procrastination at all but rather future planning.

However, be honest with yourself. Fear is sneaky, and it can make you believe that you can wait to make this decision; you don't need to do it now. This is resistance disguised as helpful advice.

Procrastination is fear—you fear getting started, you're attached to your current state, you fear letting go, you don't know what to do, you fear making a mistake, it takes too long, you worry about rejection, you're afraid of what other people will think, and a thousand other excuses for not getting started. You don't do what you know is right for you to do for whatever reason you can come up with. These are your excuses, and they don't matter.

Your excuses don't matter. The only purpose they serve is to keep you from doing what you know you need to do for yourself.

Your impetus for change must be great enough to overcome your resistance. Fear staying the same. Fear being in this same place ten years from now still deliberating, hoping, wishing, wondering . . . Ten years is a long time. If you get started now, imagine where you could be if you use the next ten years wisely.

Escaping into Fantasyland

Relaxation is essential to rejuvenate ourselves. Many of us do not do enough to relax and unwind from the stressors of life and work. We need to take time to be in nature, to exercise, to play games, and to participate in hobbies or other fun activities. You deserve time to relax and unwind at the end of a busy day.

However, resistance can show up as an excessive use of recreational or leisure activities. Escape and avoidance techniques can take many different forms. You might choose any of a myriad of substances to disconnect and forget for a while. Or you could lose yourself in food, work, reading, video games, sex, social media, or shopping.

Fantasyland is where you escape. It is your personal mental getaway. After all, you run around crazed all day, and when you come home, you crash and look for ways to escape. By escaping, you don't do what you want to do and don't enjoy the results you want. This is why you aren't looking for that new job. This is why you don't exercise. This is why you can't get your novel started. This is why your relationships are not as fulfilling as you would like them to be.

This is also your excuse. You are so busy running around putting out fires all day that you do not make time for the really important things. Or you are so lost in your escape and avoidance activity that you have become disconnected from yourself and your reality. Escape and avoidance provide only a temporary relief from your reality, and then, when you are faced with reality once again, you must face the frustration, disappointment, and anger that you have for not doing something different. It is a vicious cycle.

There is a balance between relaxing and partaking in rejuvenating activities and staying true to your goals, those things you would like to improve upon in your life.

Notice the ways in which you practice escaping and avoiding. Awareness gives you the power to choose a different path for yourself. Starting with chapter 7, where we explore the importance of commitment, you will learn what it will take to make the changes you want. For now, look for the ways in which you escape, uncover what you might be avoiding, and pay attention to where you may be giving yourself a hard time.

The Role of Drama

Drama keeps us from facing our resistance and fear. It is another game the mind plays to amuse us, trap us, and keep us from facing the real issues. We are so busy managing the chaos and dealing with the emotional highs and lows that we do not take the time to focus on ourselves and our happiness. We have forgotten joy, peace, and just being in the moment and instead are lost in the busyness and doing that we humans do and believe we are supposed to do.

Problems are dramatized on television, in movies, and in stories to get us excited and fearful, and to provide entertainment. Some people are addicted to drama and enjoy embellishing and exaggerating stories to gain attention. The news is designed to stir emotions in the audience, which means they usually emphasize stories about what is going wrong, showing people at the lowest points in their lives, and pointing out the negatives in people's lives. Rarely do we hear about things that are going well.

This can be a fun way to spend time. Drama is, in fact, entertainment. People often share stories about their experiences or about people in their workplace. And it can be interesting to listen to. Drama is the emotional engagement that occurs when sharing stories. A good story can entice you, so you become enraptured and captivated by it. You might share in the person's frustration, aggravation, or even excitement. Listening to emotional stories all day, every day, however, can be energy depleting.

We create drama when we catastrophize, making the situation the worst possible thing imaginable. The emotional upset increases as the individual focuses on the problem and how it makes them feel, how horrible it is, how much that person has endured. This focus on the emotion and the story increases the intensity of the emotion when what would better serve them would be to move through the emotional torrent, just be with it for a moment, and then seek a solution. When the person is not interested in solving their dilemma or coming up with options for improving the situation or doing something different, then the story becomes the attraction. The emotions in the story are the drama, and that has an impact on you as the listener.

Emotions require our attention. They are internal messages that bring our attention to something. So when you take in the emotional drama created by others, or if you create drama rather than managing situations thoughtfully, the drama causes angst and adds unnecessary stress to your life. The emotional highs and lows created by drama will drain you and distract you from your goal.

Drama does not equate to living a great life. In fact, most people who seek better living want more peace and less drama, although they may not know how to avoid it since for many people it is a way of life.

Give up your attachment to drama and chaos in order to create the space for change. So long as you live with drama, you will not have the time or the mental energy to focus on your vision.

Consider the role that drama plays in your life. What purpose does it serve? What do you gain by having a life filled with drama? Is there some need you have that drama satisfies for you? Such personal needs may include the need for attention, recognition, acknowledgment, acceptance, or importance.

Personal needs are habits of thought that guide your behavior, producing certain results in order to fill this void you feel (hence, the term "need"). Often, in order to feel satisfied, you behave in ways that do not represent you at your best. You chase something in order to feel whole. But they are illusions; after all, you already are whole and complete.

We all do have personal needs for attention and love and to be heard and respected and recognized. Instead of acting out fantasies or creating drama, recognize your needs and then take responsibility for getting them met. A coach or counselor can help you with this. In this way, you face your needs head-on and get them met on your own terms, safely and respectfully.

Knowing, accepting, and honoring yourself are the foundation for personal development. In my first book, *The Journey Called YOU,* I provide readers with the roadmap for learning how to live in self-discovery and acceptance. Increasing your level of self-awareness and learning skills for self-mastery are helpful for creating the changes you want.

* * *

Drama, along with self-criticism and harsh judgment, procrastination, and struggle are resistance behaviors. And they are all grounded in fear. There is one more barrier to change, and that is discouragement. Let's dive into that one next.

CHAPTER 6

DEAL WITH DISCOURAGEMENT

---

*"In spite of everything, I shall rise again: I will take up
my pencil, which I have forsaken in my great discouragement,
and I will go on with my drawing."*

—Vincent Van Gogh

Welcome to the Gap

Change is hard because it takes time. Well, it's not that it takes time and that's a bad thing; it's neither good nor bad. It just is what it is, and you don't like it. You have your own ideas about how long things should take to accomplish. Things may take too long or longer than you are willing to wait. You are impatient and become anxious. You want what you want when you want it, and you don't like delays. When it takes longer than you expect, you get discouraged.

At some point during the process of change, you believe that you should be there already. Why is it taking so long? Your ideas of how long it should take are distorted. You may start to doubt the possibility of success. If you succumb to this thinking, you may become

77

depressed. Depression is energy draining. If sustained long enough, you will give up and turn back.

Discouragement often sets in along your journey in the second phase of change, when you are in the "middle" and feeling disoriented. What *was* is over, but the beginning of what's to come—your vision—isn't here yet. You are wandering down the middle path, waiting and hoping and taking steps to create the change, but feeling like it's just not happening.

In fact, many people believe that if you envision something, you should create a dream board with pictures, and if you hope and pray enough, then you will get what you want. This is a great idea if you use the vision board to bring the ideas into focus and start doing what needs to be done to attain what you want in that vision. Without action, however, nothing happens. You wait for things to change, hoping and praying, but to no avail. Frustration and anger set in, you become discouraged and resolved to give up.

Of course, you have not yet done the work required to achieve the desired outcome. If you had, your results would reflect that.

People look for shortcuts to success, which can only lead to disappointment as they fall short of the promises for inflated outcomes. The sheer number of get-rich-quick schemes available demonstrates my point. Our society touts instant gratification and a get-it-now mentality.

Sometimes, you have unrealistic expectations as to what it actually takes to achieve the desired results. Operating under the notion that you don't have to do the work, you may still expect to reap the rewards. In this case, you don't understand what it actually takes to succeed. You have not yet learned the steps required to achieve success.

At some point in our lives, we've all been there. Success was elusive until we did the necessary work.

The idea that success should be handed to you on a silver platter, all wrapped up with a bow, causes a sense of entitlement. The entitlement mentality goes something like this:

I have an idea of how life should be. I have a vision for success. I dream of a better life, a loving relationship, a thinner body, a particular job. It should be this way because this is what I want, and this is what I expect. Then I open my eyes and reality hits. Where is that rich bank account? Where is that amazing relationship or that ideal job? I dreamed it; it should be here!

This sense of entitlement causes you to become very frustrated when you cannot achieve the results you want. Your ideas about what it takes and the reality of what it takes to achieve those results are disproportionate.

The entitlement mentality leads to discouragement.

Sometimes, you are ready and willing to do the work, and you go after your goal with vigor, but the ideas you have regarding how long it will take to achieve the desired results are inconsistent. You become frustrated and angry when you don't experience results in the amount of time you believe is reasonable. Unclear about how long it will take to achieve what you want, you become discouraged.

There is a gap between your fantasy and reality, and this gap creates your discontent.

The Problem with Expectations

Somewhere along your journey, you created expectations. Your mind formed ideas about how long it should take to achieve success. You may or may not be aware that your ideas about how long something should take to accomplish are not practical or realistic. Expectations for timelines are guesses; they can be—and often are—wrong.

Expectations set you up for frustration and discontent. You want something to happen quicker than is possible or probable so you tell yourself you "can't" or that something is "hard." You create stories about it, and the more you say it over and over again, the more you believe it. You are, in essence, creating self-fulfilling prophecies. Things seem hard because that is how you think and talk about it.

Your thoughts have a huge impact on the reality you create for yourself and how you feel about your reality.

This relationship to time is tricky. It is not wrong to have guessed incorrectly about how long something takes to come to fruition. The sooner you can accept your situation without the emotional upset, the easier it is for you to adjust your expectations to something more reasonable.

The struggle in your mind is the difference or the gap between what you want—what you expect—and your reality. How much difficulty you have with this gap can be evidenced by your behaviors.

Temper Tantrums

Having expectations, setting deadlines, and creating timelines are helpful. They are guides for your planning process. They provide the structure for the changes you wish to make. But when your expectation is threatened, when you are wrong and attached to being right, you can become very angry and upset. This often looks like a two-year-old stomping their feet during a temper tantrum (never a pretty sight).

You expect to lose ten pounds in a month. You become very angry when, after thirty days, you have only lost three pounds. Realistically, this is appropriate weight loss (especially since you cheated, remember? And you weren't as faithful to those daily workouts). But you become extremely upset. You complain to anyone who will listen. Discouragement sets in, and you give up.

What about looking for love? You think that if you sign up for a dating service, it should take a few months to find your true love. Or perhaps you believe that a reality show that offers a woman ten men to choose from will be able to find her best friend and she'll learn to love one of them for the rest of her life.

People seeking employment often have distorted views of how long it should take to find their next position, especially when changing careers. Many factors go into finding the right position, and much depends on the economy, the unemployment rate, supply of and demand for people who are seeking the same type of work, industry, and so on. How long will it take on average to find new employment today given the current state of affairs?

What's the expectation, and what is the realistic or practical outcome?

When the result you expect does not happen as you think it should, you become upset. You may blame the dating service. *It doesn't work! Nothing works. See, there are no good matches out there for me.* And you stop looking. Perhaps you resign yourself to being alone. You become depressed and lonely. And the anger remains.

After some time, you may try again with a new dating service, but unless you change how you think about and approach the dating process, you will find yourself recreating the same result because of your expectations about finding a mate.

Honestly, no one can answer the question for you about how long it will take. There is no one answer because each of us is different. Focus on getting ready for the love of your life to enter instead of complaining that they are not yet here.

Expectations lend themselves to emotional reactions when they are not met. When you experience disappointment or anger or frustration, consider your expectations. Emotions are wonderful messengers providing you with information that needs to be examined, preferably before your emotions take you for a ride. What were you thinking about how long this would take? What did you want to have happen? Were your expectations reasonable and realistic? Now that it did not happen as you intended, is there something you need to accept or change? How might you respond?

Initial failures and setbacks are to be expected. The old habit continues to try to do its job and keeps you behaving as you have always done. Initially, you will forget this new course and slip back into your old behaviors from time to time, especially if you are emotional or stressed. Times like these require awareness and grace. Notice what has occurred, give yourself grace, and practice forgiveness. This is what self-compassion looks like. Then, keep going, keep trying, and work through the discouragement.

Disappointment is a response to an unmet expectation; otherwise, there would be no reason to feel disappointed. Anger signifies that there is something that needs to be acknowledged—there has been a trespass of some kind, a disparity between what you wanted and what happened. What truth do you need to face? Only by acknowledging the truth can you then make better choices about your response as opposed to blowing up and allowing the anger to take charge. (This does not mean you have to like the truth. That is judgment. This is about acknowledging reality as it is.)

Be aware of and pay attention to your emotions. Question the emotions' message and realize that perhaps it is not possible to lose that much weight in that amount of time. Or perhaps you have gained muscle from your workouts, your clothes are fitting looser, and, after doing some research, you decide to set a more realistic and appropriate health goal that includes factors other than just weight. Perhaps the job you are seeking requires a skillset that you have not yet mastered, and the opportunity here is for you to develop additional skills. You might want to seek out a mentor, ask for a stretch goal at work, or take a class. Realize that just because you have not yet advanced in your career, that doesn't mean it won't happen; it just hasn't happened *yet*. It is not yet time.

I once heard that our prayers are answered in one of three ways:

1. Yes! You've got it!
2. It's not time yet.
3. There is something better in store for you.

You need not be religious to pray or to believe that there are forces in the universe that are greater than yourself.

Recognize that when you don't get what you want, there is a reason, even though you may not know what that reason is. *Why didn't I get that job? Why didn't that date turn into something more?* The answer is that there may be something better in store for you, or it may not be the right time. For whatever reason, it wasn't right for you right now; perhaps it was a blessing in disguise, and you have been spared from a bad situation. Trust and have faith that if you continue to respect yourself and walk your path, the right person, job, or resource will materialize in due time.

Expectations are not wrong or bad; just don't become attached to expectations as being truth. They are just ideas or best guesses.

The Meaning of Time

There is a reason you don't just blink and have what you want presented to you upon opening your eyes. Life prepares you. There are things you need to learn, do, and experience. You are growing and being primed.

Time tests your resolve and your level of commitment. If you really want this, it will happen if you "keep on keeping on," but you cannot know how long it will take.

It will take as long as it takes.

Along the way, you are learning ways to be better, to improve yourself. You are preparing yourself for this change to be permanent. There are internal changes that occur before the external change. You become a new person on your path to achieving what you desire, and you develop the characteristics and attributes you will need to succeed. It is in this way that you are prepared to handle the new situation because you are new and different too (more on this in chapter 9).

There are other things being prepared, too, besides you. Many factors need to be woven together and built, to which you are completely oblivious. For example, when I began the journey toward attracting my life partner, I had no idea how long it would be before I would meet

"Mr. Right." I also wasn't really concerned about it. I put an action plan together and began working on the plan.

I went through a lot of changes during that period of time that were preparing me for entering into, creating, and then maintaining an amazing relationship. I had much to learn. But so did Lou, the man I was to marry. There were things he needed to do and ways he needed to grow and change before he would be ready for me and our relationship. We could never have known this consciously.

We act in ways to care for and respect the best of ourselves and carry with us the faith and trust that if we do what we need to do, then the rest will take care of itself.

That's how it works when we focus on ourselves as opposed to forcing our will, wanting our way, and fighting reality. It is much easier when we focus on bettering ourselves and let go of trying to change things over which we have no control.

I Want It NOW!

On your journey of a thousand miles, you don't know how long it will take to achieve the results you seek in part because the perspective you have is so limited. It is hard to zoom out to take the helicopter view of life and properly judge how long you need to travel to get to the end point.

People generally don't have a long-term mentality. We tend think for the short term and the impact it has today, this week, this month, or this year (if we consider the impact at all). We are less likely to think about how the actions we take today will impact us ten or twenty years from now.

By thinking and wishing it would happen sooner, you cause yourself to be disappointed, which may lead you to quit prematurely. Change takes time. How much time may not be known; however, being unrealistic sets you up for disappointment, and that could sabotage you and your efforts.

For instance, thinking that you could reverse your debt in a month when it took you years to get indebted is unrealistic. How long it will take depends on many factors, including how much debt you have, your income, your commitment to getting out of debt and forsaking other purchases, and your other financial responsibilities. It takes several years to become debt-free. When people hear that, they meet resistance. People have difficulty seeing things over the long term; although, by doing nothing, they may never get out of debt. Some people prefer that to being without their credit cards for several years. This means that they are still committed to being in debt.

Your actions say a lot about what you are committed to (commitments are discussed in chapter 7).

Even if it were possible to get out of debt overnight, you would find yourself back in debt in no time, for you have not learned the necessary lessons to maintain a debt-free lifestyle. There is much you need to learn and unlearn to change your habits and your thought processes so that once out of debt, you behave differently and start on the path toward amassing wealth (or, at the very least, living within your means).

There are beliefs, assumptions, and behaviors that will need to change, and while you are taking the journey to eliminate your debt, you can learn those habits of thought and behavior, disconnect from your attachments to spending more than what you earn, and redefine your relationship to money. There is also a correlation between your self-esteem and money. During the time it takes you to get out of debt, you can work on improving your self-esteem and developing yourself so that you feel good about who you are rather than defining yourself by your purchases or lifestyle.

If someone had told me that it would take two years to find my soulmate and enter into a relationship, I would have been discouraged. Two years seems like a long time of focused attention and effort.

On the flip side, however, two years is nothing compared to the lifetime we will share together.

Two years is the time we needed to get our respective acts together. It was also the time needed for other factors to fall into place so that we could meet and recognize the meeting as an opportunity for a relationship.

Saving for retirement takes decades of diligent saving. Is it worth the work? Is it of greater value for you to give up spending on something today so you can save that money to ensure you can support yourself when you are older? You might respond affirmatively but knowing it and doing it are two different things.

When impatience sets in, you get discouraged. You want the change to happen sooner. You don't want to wait that long to reap the rewards. Even if you correctly estimate the amount of time it will take to achieve the results you want, you may not want it to take that long, and in your mind, you may find yourself scheming and plotting for ways you can shorten the timeframe to success.

This is something I struggle with regularly. I am aware of my tendency to be impatient. I don't like waiting for things to happen. Although this has improved as I have gotten older, I continue to be challenged with things taking too long. I have to consciously focus on the here and now and accept my reality. When I feel impatient, I shift my attention to accepting the pace of the journey. I focus on pacing myself rather than trying to learn how to wait.

Pay attention to this moment and notice when your mind starts to drift into thinking that you *should* be experiencing different results. Your thoughts are moving into the territory of not accepting reality and wanting things to be different (i.e., wishful thinking), and if you are not careful, you may experience an emotional reaction that mimics a temper tantrum.

Travel the Gap

Expectations are your guidelines for achieving success. Not good or bad, they are one way you can judge how you are doing. Keep an open mind as you set expectations so that you are realistic in your assessment.

For instance, just because you've decided it's time for change does not mean your life is instantly different. You may be different internally, but your external world isn't.

There is a gap that occurs between the time when you set your mind on change and when the change actually becomes reality. The internal shift takes place first, and then your external world changes to align with your new mindset.

This gap is where we become frustrated. After all, you are ready; why can't you just be there already!

It doesn't work that way. You have to travel the gap. There are no shortcuts to success. Lessons must be learned along the way.

- Figure out what it takes to travel the gap from where you are now to where you want to be,
- Set realistic expectations for achieving and accomplishing the steps required to get to the other side, and then,
- Take the first step!

Sometimes, you set realistic expectations, but they turn out to be unrealistic. Be open to this and make adjustments. Reflection of your journey is essential. What stops you from succeeding? What are the stories you tell yourself? Explore the thoughts, beliefs, and rationalizations that guide your behavior. Often a coach or other professional is necessary for this type of exploration. It can be challenging to examine your thinking on your own.

For example, Betsy (not her real name) was discouraged that she was unable to meet her monthly sales goals. She accepted goals based on what she perceived was expected of her, not taking into account that she had other responsibilities (like kids and a house to manage) and that she preferred to balance her work with her home life. Month after month, she fell short and was embarrassed in front of her team.

In this case, Betsy was working toward unrealistic expectations but did not realize it. In doing so, she was setting herself up for failure.

She finally readjusted her goals to be more realistic to fit her lifestyle and the time she was willing to put into sales. Now she meets her goals every month, and it feels great!

Once she made adjustments to her expectations for more reasonable outcomes, Betsy began to play again. She enjoyed going to work. She was successful at achieving her goals each month, was less stressed, and received praise and recognition from her team. And her family appreciated it too!

Other times, you set realistic expectations and something unexpected happens outside your control. For example, you are ready to retire, but with a downturn in the economy, you are nervous about your level of savings. You decide it is best to continue working for another few years.

You can only do what you can control—your thoughts, your emotions, and your actions. Focusing on being frustrated and getting angry about things outside your control will not serve you and will increase your stress levels and your discontent. Take back your power and focus your attention and actions on what you can control, do the best you can, and make adjustments when necessary.

You cannot control the outcome, only the process and the actions you take to move you toward your destination. Ask what needs to be accepted about your reality, set different goals, and change course if needed.

The Long and Winding Road

Time is relative. To one person, taking two weeks for vacation is an appropriate amount of time to relax and unwind; to another person, taking that much time seems completely unreasonable. It all depends upon how you think about it. To one person something may be hard; to someone else, it's a piece of cake.

Consider this: Driving to your destination, you are unsure of where you are going. You pay attention to every light, every turnoff, every mile marker. The trip seems to go on forever. The return trip, however, is easy because you already know your way.

When we examine even the tiniest thing with such great detail and focus, it becomes bigger and seems to take longer. It is our perception that is different. Driving to your destination, you have to use your mind's energy to focus. On the way home, you relax and enjoy the drive.

On the way to your destination, you become frustrated. Negative thoughts of self-doubt, pity, hopelessness, and despair creep into your consciousness. You wonder if you'll ever get there. You only see the long road ahead of you. Focused on the fact that you are not there yet, you worry about being late. Your inner critic kicks into high gear, putting you down and berating you for not starting out sooner on your journey. You may become enraged, angry at yourself and at others for getting in your way.

The same is true in life. When you only focus on the road ahead, you shift away from the present and move into resistance. You begin to lose faith in your ability to achieve the results you desire. This is how it begins; your resolve and commitment to change are being tested. Will you give in? Will you allow yourself to drown in the pools of discouragement? Or will you learn the ways to take back your power and move forward toward success?

*   *   *

Change is H.A.R.D. Habits, Attachments, Resistance, and Discouragement are ways that your mind tricks you and toys with you. They are very difficult to navigate. Now that you understand how the mind works, the following eight simple strategies will help you to approach change from a different perspective so you can take an easier path. Use your mind to assist you in making change happen as opposed to working against you and fighting you when you want to change. Yes, change requires work, but that doesn't mean you cannot be in control and enjoy the process. When you know the steps, anything can become *easier*.

CHAPTER 7

STRATEGY 1:
COMMIT TO CHANGE

---

*"I know the price of success: dedication, hard work,
and an unremitting devotion to the things
you want to see happen."*

—Frank Lloyd Wright

Commitment Unlocks the Door to Success

You are committed to something. Until now, you have been committed to your old life: being unhappy and undervalued at work, being overweight or indebted, holding on to the pain you experienced as a child or from a previous marriage. You have been committed to the story and to maintaining the status quo, and that has been fueling your attachments.

Now, you want a better you and a better life. You want to retire with enough money to feel comfortable. You want to let go of the weight you've been carrying around with you. You want to experience a deeper, more connected, and more passionate relationship with your spouse—or perhaps you want to find a spouse to experience this deep connection with. Perhaps the connection you desire is with your parents or friends—a community of people to share life with. Or perhaps you want that promotion or raise or to move across the country.

Commitment is your strategy for success. You must commit to making this change to create a better life. By committing, you become steadfast and dedicated. Failure is not an option. Your commitment causes a mental shift that reinforces your new path.

When you commit, you take a stand for something that is meaningful to you. If you are committed, then you will take the necessary steps to achieve success. You will:

- Envision success. You'll be serious about achieving the end result.

- Create a plan of action so you are clear about the steps required to get there.

- Take the actions required in order to turn your vision into reality. You'll be internally motivated to take action toward your goal.

- Let go of the "old you" and develop into the "new you" so that you are prepared for the success to come. The person you become when you achieve success will be different. Commitment helps you embrace and accept this new you now.

- Let go of old, limiting beliefs and strengthen your self-esteem. You'll learn more positive and empowering beliefs and use positive self-talk.

- Persist when times get rough. Without persistence, you may give up, as many people do. Commitment includes persisting to the end.

- Get the needed support—a coach, mentor, or friend that keeps you focused and on track until you reach your destination.

- Do whatever it takes because you are committed to reaching your goal.

With commitment, you are respectful in your interactions and use empathy to improve your relationships with your boss, staff, colleagues, spouse, mother, or children.

With commitment, you are willing to learn what it takes to get promoted—even return to college for additional education if needed. You'll do whatever it takes.

With commitment, your dreams become reality.

Without commitment, it remains a dream. A wish. A hope.

And without commitment, you will torment yourself with negative comments: *See, I'll never get that promotion. I will never have an amazing relationship. I will never lose those twenty pounds.* Without commitment, your mind will run wild with limiting beliefs and negativity, making it impossible for success.

You want a new life; now you must ask yourself some tough questions about whether you are ready to commit:

- *Do I have the necessary resources—the time, energy, and finances—to complete this vision or goal?*
- *Is now the right time for this goal?*
- *Is it worthwhile? Why? What will I gain? How will this add value to my life?*
- *What will I have to give up or let go of?*
- *Am I prepared for what I will gain as a result?*
- *Is this something I "should" do or something I really want to do?*
- *Am I ready to take this on, to give up how I've been living in order to go after something new?*

Many times, people decide to embark upon a path because it is the "right thing to do." But you will not commit to doing whatever it takes if it's not what you really want to do. You won't be able to commit to your new life. You'll silently and secretly hang on to the old story, and you will sabotage your success.

If, after doing the due diligence, you decide you don't want to commit, let yourself off the hook! Give yourself permission to stay as you are. It's okay! Just be willing to accept the consequences of this course of action. Don't continue to complain. Accept this path with full responsibility and be curious about why you are so committed to remaining on this course. Be curious as to why you are not ready. What is your story? What are you committed to now, and how is this adding value to you? What are you gaining by keeping things as they are?

You must be gaining something, even if it's embarrassing or negative, or you would do something else. Take the time to figure it out. If you cannot commit to change, then commit to figuring out what you do want to be committed to rather than just doing what you've always done, unconsciously accepting that "it's just the way I am."

Your power is in your ability to choose. But you cannot choose if you are not aware of your choices. Don't just live blindly attached to the way things have been.

If you're not yet ready to commit but still want to change, then do the work to become ready for change as opposed to pushing a goal on yourself that you are not yet ready to tackle. This will make life easier and less stressful rather than setting you up for struggle and failure. And when you are ready to commit to a change, go for it with everything you've got!

Add Value to Your Life

To succeed at your goal, choose the right things for the right reasons. How will this change add value to your life? How will it increase the quality of your life? What is the significance of working toward this goal now?

It is common in our society to title projects, programs, and even our personal goals using the words "anti," "quit," or "stop" along with the very word that we want to eliminate, such as "anti-drug," "quit smoking," "lose weight," "anti-bullying," "anti-violence." In these cases, the mind focuses on the noun (drug, violence, weight), not the descriptor (anti, stop). Negative titles hurt us by keeping our attention on the very thing we want to eradicate. Our thoughts create our reality: what we think about, we bring about. Hence, we bring about more of the very things we wish to change.

Language has an extraordinarily powerful impact. Because our minds cannot process negatives, don't focus your goal or commitment on "losing" or "stopping" anything. Change your description for change to make it positive so you focus on what you want to gain rather than what you want to lose. In order to stop smoking, for example, you must change your identity to become someone who loves and appreciates your health and lungs.

The words chosen for your title or goal are what you focus on and make more of. If you received feedback that you can be abrupt, for example, instead of wording your goal to be less abrupt, you might state the goal as a desire to strengthen your relationships with others or become a better communicator. Instead of your goal being to stop interrupting, you might rephrase it as becoming a good listener, someone who asks more questions and pauses before responding. If you are looking to lose weight, for example, focus instead on what you want to gain—health, fitness, endurance, energy, control, confidence, strength, or even a better shape or sexier figure. The scale can be used as a measure to show you how well you are progressing in addition to other measures, such as how your clothes fit, your energy level, strength level, endurance, blood work, or body measurements.

If you want to make real and sustainable change, then choose your words carefully so that your attention focuses on creating the very thing you do want and not what you don't want. Use language that motivates you and moves you toward what you desire rather than away from something. State your commitment in such a way that you focus on what you want to gain rather than what you want to eliminate from your life.

Leave Your Excuses at the Door

Your actions speak volumes about what you are committed to. For instance, you say you value your health and want to live a long life to enjoy your grandkids, but you make excuses. You don't have the time to work out. You don't plan your meals. You eat a lot of fast food, and you haven't been to the doctor for a checkup in years. What do these behaviors tell you about what you are committed to?

Behaviors speak volumes. If you do not experience the results you seek, the answer lies in your actions. Observe your behaviors, listen to your comments and complaints, and identify the behaviors that might need to be changed. Your actions produce your results, but the thoughts, feelings, beliefs, and assumptions all produce the behaviors. If you want to change, first notice the behavior, then you can unpack the beliefs that support that behavior.

Another example comes from one of my clients who stated that she wanted a more romantic relationship with her spouse, but she consistently found ways to put him down and often pointed out to him the things she didn't like. She didn't appreciate what her husband did for her and was only able to see what she perceived was wrong. When it was time for bed, she found herself disinterested and too tired for sexual contact and intimacy. Of course, his behavior was similar to hers. They had created this dynamic over the years. Both were responsible.

As humans, we make all sorts of excuses and justifications, we rationalize and defend, we apologize and explain. Our brains look for ways to make sense of the information we receive. Are you making excuses for your choices rather than accepting responsibility for them? Are you seeking some kind of validation?

Sometimes, we make excuses and defend ourselves out of guilt. We feel badly about something and try to make ourselves feel better. In this way, we avoid admitting the mistake or accepting responsibility for what we have done.

Sometimes, we make excuses and defend ourselves to avoid doing what we know we need to do for ourselves. "I should go to the gym (to the doctor, on vacation, etc.) but I'm just so busy."

Other times we make excuses because that's what we always do, and we may not realize we do it. It's a habit.

The explanations often pile up. If you listen, you will hear yourself give numerous excuses for why life is not the way it "should" be.

The key is to notice when you are making excuses, justifying your behavior, defending yourself, or rationalizing something. Notice, and then ask yourself what is really going on for you.

- *Are you feeling guilty?* Is this real guilt because you made a mistake, or is it an old reaction from childhood? Are you accepting responsibility for something you have done, or are you assuming responsibility for someone else's wrongdoing?

- *Is there something that you need to correct or be honest about, difficult as it may be to face?* In what way(s) might you be lying to yourself? What we resist persists until we are able to face the truth of the situation and our contribution to it. Maybe you are afraid to take a vacation because of the work you will miss. Is that a fear of missing out or is there something else going on for you?

- *Do you simply need to give yourself permission to make this choice?* For instance, after being in debt for so long, Dominique still feels guilty when she goes to purchase something for herself even though she is using her available cash and it is something she could really use. Although she made bad choices in the past, she now must learn to trust herself to make good decisions about money.

- *Do you need to stop "should-ing" yourself, reevaluate your priorities, and set better goals?* For example, you complain that you don't have time to go to the gym. Maybe you don't like going to a gym for fear of being judged. There are other ways to incorporate movement and exercise into your daily routine. Accept responsibility for your choices. You will do what you perceive is of greatest value to you. If you do not work out, it's not because you don't have time; it's because you don't make the time. It is not a priority for you right now. Instead of the excuses, decide what role you want fitness to play in your life, and if it is important to you, then set a realistic goal for that.

- *Do you feel the need to defend or explain yourself?* Defensiveness is a sign of a fragile or hurting self-esteem seeking value and validation. As a mature, responsible adult, there is little you will do that requires defending to anyone else. You are accountable to yourself. Operate in a way that reflects your ability to make good choices on your own behalf. If you struggle, then do what you must to learn the skills to make better decisions and build trust in yourself.

Bottom line:

- Notice throughout your day the excuses you make and the explanations you have for the things you do or don't do.
- Accept responsibility for your actions, stop making excuses, and make choices that honor you.
- If you want to do something different, then reconsider your priorities and set a different, more realistic goal.

It is a much happier, more peaceful, and more powerful place to be when you stop rationalizing your behavior and start accepting responsibility for it instead. If you're making excuses, you have not yet committed.

Stop making excuses. If you are not yet committed, accept where you are on your journey; you're not yet ready. When you are committed, you will do whatever it takes to make your life great. Stop settling for less. Every day is a new opportunity to do something different.

Choose What Is of Value to You

Much like your commitment, knowing what is of greatest value to you—what is most important to you—provides you with direction and focus for your actions. Ask yourself often, "What do I value most in this situation?" This will help you to take actions that support what is most important to you.

For example, you may routinely get into arguments. Next time this begins, take a moment to stop and ask yourself what's important to you here: is it more important to be right or to have a good relationship with that person? Being right is about getting your way, forcing your personal views on another person rather than honoring and respecting the different ways people see the world. Caring about the relationship means understanding and accepting those differences and being willing and open to hear another person's point of view. You don't have to agree, but listening without judgment enables the person to feel seen, heard, and valued as a human being.

We get what we give. So if you want more love, show more love. If you want more respect, show more respect (to others and to yourself). If something is not quite right in your relationship, address it. Don't let things fester. This is how our relationships deteriorate over time. If you value your relationship, take better care of it.

If you don't stop to ask yourself what is important to you, you will continue to recreate the same dynamic, and nothing will change.

Most of us go through life half awake. We don't pay attention, and we focus on things that are not really important. We are busy, you see, and when we are busy, we don't take a moment to ask what is really important. Instead, we react as we always do. We grab that cupcake. We raise our voices. We act out of habit.

In any given moment, stop to ask yourself what is of greatest value to you. Check in with your new commitment for change. Will the choice you are about to make move you closer to your goal? Does it add value and help you develop the characteristics you believe are important for success? Does it help you become the person you want to be?

Knowing what you value in each moment will inform your behavior and help you feel better about yourself and your relationships. Why? Because you will behave differently. With each action you take that feels good, that honors you, and that is of value to you, you increase your self-confidence and feel more connected to others and to the universe at large. (For more information about how to become more self-aware, accept yourself, and make choices that honor you, pick up a copy of my first book, *The Journey Called YOU: A Roadmap to Self-Discovery and Acceptance*.)

Your life and your actions are a reflection of what you value. Ask yourself: "What can I do right now that would add the greatest value?" Is what you are doing, or about to do, adding value and moving you toward your vision for success, or is it depleting you and keeping you stuck? Is it coming from your strength or from resistance and fear?

Why Change? And Why Change Now?

Why do you want to embark upon this change now? You have to know why you want to do this. There has to be a really good reason for rocking your world; so big, in fact, that it provides you with the motivation you need to sustain you along the way.

Commitment, after all, is not something you do once and you're done. Your commitment will be tested again and again and again. You will need to recommit at every turn along the way.

Be honest with yourself. Why do you want this? What is significant about making this change? If you make this change, what will it do for you and your life? How will it add value? What will you gain as a result of this change?

Also consider what you might lose as a result. What will you need to give up? Are you prepared to let go?

What is important to you about this? Is this important enough that you are willing to do whatever it takes to achieve the results you seek?

You have to make the change for you: not for your kids, your boss, or your spouse. For you.

It cannot be a *should*, something you should do because _____ (fill in the blank). If you *should* do it but you don't want to, you will struggle, sabotage your efforts, and fail. Get honest with yourself and give up on *should*s. Focus instead on getting ready.

There has to be a reason, and it has to be a good one. It can be simple, like your health or wanting to make more money or become a better leader. It need not be complicated or fancy. But it needs to be a strong motivator to help you break through the habits and attachments that you have now, the habits that will fight to keep you doing things the way you have been for so long.

Why is this important to you *now*? You may hold on to goals from when you were young, thinking you still want it. Is the goal outdated? Is it something you really want for yourself at this time in your life, and is now the right time to embark upon this change?

When you know why this change is important, then this is your purpose statement, the reason that makes accomplishing this change meaningful and powerful. With this purpose statement, you increase your confidence and are ready to take the next step.

Commitment forces you to question your thinking and your beliefs. Only by examining the thoughts that guide your actions can you be in charge of them. Observe your thoughts. Pay attention so you become aware of the thoughts and the stories that guide your behavior and run your life. Then you can choose better, more helpful, and empowering thoughts and create new stories to tell yourself to reinforce the behaviors that support your success.

Commitment shakes these thoughts loose so you can question them. Will the thought or belief support you in your new life? Will it bring you closer to your goal or keep you stuck? Is it of value to you?

What choice could you make right now that would add value to you and move you closer to your desired outcome?

The work you do to arrive at your commitment must continue at every step along the way. You must commit and recommit at every stage and at every step on your journey. There will be forces that will attempt to shake you from your goal. Your commitment will keep you focused and motivated. This is why it is important for you to know why you are doing this and be clear about the value of making this change in your life now.

Although the process of committing may not seem easy, being committed makes it easier for you to take the steps required in order to change. After all, you are committed to something. It's important to know what you are committed to and to use that as a strategy for achieving what you desire. Your behavior and your results point to your current commitments. So if you are not achieving the results you really want, this is a red flag that you can use to help you choose to commit to something new.

*   *   *

The strategies all work together to help you achieve your ambitions. In strategy 2, I ask you to look into your crystal ball and envision what you want for yourself. What do you see for your future?

CHAPTER 8

STRATEGY 2:
ENVISION A BETTER FUTURE

---

*". . . A dream, backed by an unrelenting will to attain it,
is truly a reality with an imminent arrival."*

—Anthony Robbins

An Easier, Softer Way

Breaking habits and creating new ones is hard. It requires attention and focus, repetition, and consistency over a period of time. Depending upon many factors (i.e., what the habit is, how often you access it, how attentive you are to making the change, etc.), it can take days, weeks, or even months to create a habit, and even then, it can be easy to slip back into the old ones.

You will need to learn new skills and new ways of thinking in order to create new habits that will support your success with the change you wish to make.

People struggle to learn new things, and they force themselves to take actions that seem like chores. If you hate what you are doing, you will resist and get discouraged. You won't follow through, and you are bound to fail.

Instead of focusing on changing bad habits and learning new ones, even though in the end that is exactly what will happen, begin by focusing your attention on envisioning the future you want to create. We begin with new thoughts.

Close your eyes and envision your new reality. What do you want? Dream about how you want your life to be different. What do you see in this vision? Describe it in detail. Write it down. Add to it regularly and re-read it every day—as often as you can.

Imagine how you are behaving. What are some of the things you are doing? Who are you with? How are you interacting? How are you different from the person you are today? Identify the characteristics that are important to you in this future vision. Are they different from what's important to you today?

How do you feel in your vision? Are you having fun? Are you happy, excited, relaxed, and peaceful? Are you more confident? How is this different from the way you generally feel today?

Once you can identify what you want, what you are doing, and how you want to feel, you may want to make a vision board with a collage of pictures, words, and phrases to help you visualize what you want to create and remind you of what you are working toward. Some people prefer a narrated version and write their vision in a journal. Others create a mind movie using software to put images to music.

The person you are in your vision is not the same person you are today. Spend some time getting to know this new reflection of you. Identify the qualities and characteristics you display. How are you different in this new future you envision?

Do you find as you read through this exercise that you are experiencing any resistance? Do you think this is corny? Do you believe that this is not important or won't work? Do you have any other negative or resistant thoughts about the visioning process?

Pay attention. It is important that you recognize this resistance and any negative beliefs. These thoughts are sabotaging you and keeping you from achieving what you want. And they are just thoughts. They are not bigger than you; you are bigger than your thoughts.

Nonsmokers Don't Smoke

It was the year 1994, the year between my first and second year of nursing school. I could not seem to put "smoking" and "nurse" in the same sentence. It was out of integrity for me, and I knew I had to stop smoking before I graduated.

So, when I decided to quit smoking, I did what most people try to do: I quit. I picked a day, and just stopped.

It was horrible. I was miserable. I thought about smoking all the time. For two weeks, I was a mess. I was stressed out, struggling, irritable. I couldn't do it! I still wanted to quit, but I had to accept that I was not yet ready, and I gave myself permission to start smoking again.

But something had changed for me, and I wasn't smoking as much. Instead of my usual number of cigarettes, I only smoked enough to get through the urges. It didn't taste good anymore; I didn't like the smell. It was a habit: habits of thought and beliefs with emotional attachments and habitual behaviors. Nicotine is physiologically addicting; however, with a short half-life of two to three hours (a half-life is how long it takes the body to clear half of the substance), it is completely metabolized and removed from the body in less than a week.

I spent the next few months working on my mind. I envisioned my life as a nonsmoker, a healthy person who cared about their lungs. How would I manage through the day without cigarettes? What would I do instead of taking smoke breaks at work? Everything I associated with smoking had to be examined and redefined. I needed to know life as a nonsmoker. I was committed to quitting. I valued my health and being a nurse. Now, I just needed to learn how to be different, and I learned it first in my mind by separating everything that I normally connected with cigarettes. I cleaned out my car and then stopped smoking in the car and my home. I began doing things differently in little ways until one day, I woke up and I didn't smoke! I did not reach for a cigarette or think about reaching for one. I didn't smoke because, in my mind, I had become a nonsmoker and, you know, nonsmokers don't smoke. Now, I needed my external behaviors to catch up to my internal view of myself.

I have to admit, I was a little emotional and miserable for three days. After that, I never looked back.

In order to make a change, become a new you first in your mind. Then, start taking the actions required to become this new person. Eventually, it will become you. As Anthony Robbins states in the quote that began this chapter, the dream is an imminent reality when you are committed and unrelenting.

Whenever people mention to me that they want to "quit" smoking, I suggest they become a nonsmoker first in their mind. Then giving up cigarettes is easy because, you know, nonsmokers don't smoke!

Mental Reconditioning

In your mind, you have an image of yourself. You are conditioned to see yourself this way and to be the person you are today. You have created this image. This is your ego at work.

If you see yourself as poor or broke, then this is your self-image. You will find, with observation, that how you speak, the thoughts you think, and the things you do are all consistent with someone who is broke. Your beliefs about money—how it is earned, how hard it is to save—and your negative beliefs about rich people all coincide with your behavior, and they have created your reality.

In other words, you behave based on how you think. If you think like someone who despises money, you will repel it. When opportunities crop up to make more money or to embrace a different lifestyle, you will not recognize the opportunity and will do things to sabotage it.

The mind does not like incongruities, so if you see yourself as broke, in debt, and never having enough money, then you will behave this way to create this reality. It's a self-fulfilling prophecy. Your internal environment or thoughts must coincide with your external world. If they do not, then the subconscious mind will work hard to make it congruent, and you will begin to behave differently.

Remember this: your internal world must match your external world.

Regardless of what you want to change—perhaps you want to work fewer hours in a week, spend more time with your family, or receive a promotion, or you want to enjoy a wonderful, romantic relationship, or you want to be out of debt and comfortable in retirement—you will need to assess the mental conditioning that has created your current reality.

There is a reason you believe as you believe right now. It has served some purpose to be as you are. Respect yourself and the choices you have made in the past. This mental conditioning has helped you in some way. Perhaps it has protected you. If you have had some bad experiences in your past, the thinking processes you developed were intended to serve you, to keep you safe, to assist you.

Now, you have outgrown this thinking and you seek something new. It is time to take responsibility for new thinking and for letting go of the old thought patterns. They will not serve you where you are going.

Become a New You

Get to know who you will be when you have achieved your goal and identify the qualities of this person. Your job is to develop those qualities today so that you can become this new you.

Craft a new self-image. If you want to be different in some way, embrace the qualities of the kind of person who would have that end result. If you want to be a better leader, identify the qualities and attributes that you believe great leaders possess. Script a new story about who you are as a leader. How are you showing up? How are you behaving differently than today? How does it feel to be this new you?

If thoughts create our reality by triggering an emotional response that leads us to behave a certain way, then by crafting a new story and repeating it over and over again, you create new neurological connections in your brain. You start to believe new things about yourself. You start to act in ways that are congruent with your story. And your actions create your new reality. Your story becomes a self-fulfilling prophecy.

If you want something in your life to change, change your story.

Tell yourself a new story about how you live, about what's important to you, about your work, about the relationship you enjoy with your spouse, about your body and health, about your kids. Script a new story and create a new future.

Easy!

The key is to repeat the story over and over again. Eventually you will develop new habits of thought and new beliefs, you'll take different actions, and you'll develop the qualities and characteristics of the kind of person who would experience that which you want to have.

In other words, you walk yourself into the habits you wish to create, but you do so from the inside out rather than forcefully trying to change your habits. By having a compelling vision that excites you and by scripting a new story that becomes you, you start behaving like this new version of yourself and believing in the possibility of this becoming true. This all contributes to rewiring your brain to produce new neurological connections. You then create new habits that produce a new outcome.

When I was dating and looking for a mate, I envisioned a partnership and how wonderful it would be. I envisioned things we would be doing together, how it would feel each day to be in love and to be engaged in a passionate and loving partnership. I envisioned how we would communicate and the things we would do together.

Today, I enjoy that relationship with my husband, Lou. It has become my reality because I first envisioned what I wanted. We create and recreate each day the special reality we want for our relationship. And it all began with a thought.

The Law of Attractiveness

Visualization is only one piece of the puzzle, albeit a powerful one. These strategies work together to assist you in making a change. For instance, with my vision for a loving union, I made a list of qualities that I would need to possess in order to participate in this relationship. What would this relationship require of me? What qualities would my ideal partner look for in me? I spent time developing those qualities and working on becoming that partner. This is strategy 3: developing the characteristics you need to succeed.

This is, in essence, the Law of Attraction. We attract things into our lives because we are energetically vibrating at a certain level. The Law of Attraction allows us to accept responsibility for our lives and everything that happens to us.

I refer to it as the Law of Attractiveness because this way, you focus on becoming attractive to whatever it is you want. If you want more money, how might you need to behave differently? What qualities do people who make that amount of money possess? Go find them. Read about them. Be mentored by someone whose success you admire. Go find out what they do, how they behave, and how they think. Rich people think differently about money—about everything—than poor people.

How you identify yourself speaks volumes about where you are in the process. For example, some people who have been married a long time and then become widowed or divorced find another spouse quite quickly, while other people search endlessly for someone to love and spend years being single. Why? Why is it easy for some to find love and for others to struggle?

The difference is that some people are used to being partnered. They are programmed for it. They enjoy having a partner and being a partner. It's what they are used to. They are not attached to only having *that* partner, the one they lost. They value "partnering."

People who have been single for a long time might need to learn how to partner with someone. They are used to being single and doing things on their own. It's different to have someone with whom you share everything, and it takes some adjusting in order to feel comfortable. It can be done. I know people who partnered in marriage for the first time in their fifties after being single for decades. It requires new thoughts, new beliefs, new habits, and new behaviors.

~ * ~

Defining and becoming a new you from the inside out is another strategy for sustaining success. This is strategy 3 and is discussed in the next chapter. Once you become new, it is much harder to go back to your old ways.

Visualization allows you to dream of the new you so you can identify the attributes you will possess in this idealized future. By identifying these characteristics, you can start practicing them in your life today. As you do, you start vibrating energetically at a new level so you can attract what you want. You become attractive and worthy of what you want, and it comes into your life effortlessly.

Along the way, you become a new person, adopting new beliefs about life and what you deserve; you see yourself differently and become a better you, developing important characteristics necessary for your future. You have a new vision, which is a beacon and guiding light. You adopt new behaviors, and you create new habits.

Easy.

CHAPTER 9

STRATEGY 3: DEVELOP THE CHARACTERISTICS YOU NEED TO SUCCEED

*"Dignity consists not in possessing honors,
but in the consciousness that we deserve them."*

—Aristotle

Who Do You Want to Become?

You have a vision for change. You imagine how life will be different and how you will be different. In this vision, you are doing different things, hanging out with different people, and feeling differently about who you are. Your future self is not the same as the person you are today. You have different values and different priorities.

Your life today reflects what you value. As you embark upon a life change, while you will change your behaviors and begin doing things differently, you will also need to change how you think about yourself, what is important to you, what you value, and how you

111

approach life. Your operating system and beliefs in this new life differ from the way you live today. Depending upon the change you wish to make, new values, priorities, and attributes need to be identified and nurtured in order for you not only to create the change but to maintain the change.

For example, you want to get out of debt. In the past, you may have valued spending money, making purchases on credit, perhaps impressing other people, and gaining self-esteem by being able to purchase whatever you wanted when you felt so inclined. You were not aware of your spending habits or that spending may have been a source of self-esteem for you. You did not calculate the difference between how much you earned versus how much you spent. You may not even have been aware of how much you owed.

Then you have an awakening (a "whack" on the side of the head). Bills are piling up; you receive a notice from a collection's office or a lawyer; your mortgage is in jeopardy. Something wakes you to the reality of your situation and the need to change.

Perhaps nothing in particular startles you, but you are triggered to consider different ways of approaching money. You turn a certain age or have a new baby and realize that you want to be debt-free and have more money in savings. You want to move to a different location or across the country. You consider the actions you need to take and come up with a strategy for change.

In addition to doing different things, you will become a different person. As you begin changing behaviors, there will be a shift internally in how you think about yourself and your approach to living. What does it mean to be debt-free and financially independent? Consider the kind of person you want to become as you redefine yourself within the context of this change and then come up with a strategy for developing yourself in this way. In other words, define the attributes and characteristics of the kind of person who has what you want and then focus your attention and effort on developing those qualities.

Whatever your goal, by crafting a strategy for "being" in addition to "doing" you focus attention on developing and growing yourself so that, in essence, you become someone new along the way.

When you went to college, you dreamed of what it would be like to work in the field of your choosing. You envisioned yourself there. You envisioned yourself an "expert," someone others could count on and come to for advice. To be confident and capable, you envisioned certain qualities, and, over time, you developed those qualities.

If you want to do something different, you also have to become someone different. You cannot succeed in your quest for change if you do not change how you are being in the process. You must develop and grow; otherwise, it will not be sustainable.

It is hard when you only focus on changing habits and pushing yourself to change your behaviors. Instead, an easier way is to envision success and identify the key characteristics needed to achieve success. Practice developing those attributes, and this will lead you to success with less effort. Eventually, you will become more confident and comfortable in your new role, and you will feel as though you belong in this new life. In this way, you nurture a new inner environment, a mindset that will guide you to the change you desire.

Your inner environment is your internal dialogue, what you say to yourself—your thoughts. To create change, your internal dialogue needs to change. Get your mind on your side. Update your self-image and the story you live by. By thinking new thoughts about who you are and what's important to you, in essence, you "think" yourself into your new reality. (Yes, much like "fake it until you make it.")

As you develop the character traits needed to achieve your goal, you will easily begin to do the things that are in alignment with the attributes you are displaying, and success will be realized. Because you evolve to become someone new in the process, there is no going back, only forward. The old you gives way to unleash a newer, improved version of you.

Create a Strategy for Becoming a New You

When you see someone else enjoying the success you desire, observe them. Learn from them. Read about them. How do they behave? What do they do that is different? In addition, notice what they value. What are their priorities? What is important to them? What are the characteristics you would use to describe this kind of person?

If you want to *do* something different, you will need to *become* someone different.

For example, what are the qualities of someone who is wealthy—how do they behave differently? What do they talk about regularly when they refer to money? What is important to them? How do they treat their money? How do they treat the things they purchase with their money? Just because people spend a lot does not mean they have money; they could have a lot of debt!

Who you need to become depends upon the change you wish to make. If you want to create an amazing relationship with your spouse (or find a life partner), identify the characteristics that will be required of you. For instance, you may need to be more open with your feelings, more honest, and a better listener. You may need to communicate effectively by identifying your needs and asking for your needs to be met as opposed to expecting your partner to be a really good mind reader. You also may need to be open to new possibilities and not be so attached to your way being the right way. What else might need to change in order for you to become a good life partner?

Perhaps you want to become a better leader or be promoted to lead others. Consider the best boss you ever had. What were the qualities that they displayed that made them effective at leading others? How might you adopt those qualities and develop them for yourself?

In order to adopt a healthier lifestyle, there are certain characteristics that you will need to embrace, such as choosing healthy food options, making physical activity a priority, and valuing your health above all. What is your vision for someone who is healthy? How do they plan their meals? What food choices do they make? What role does exercise or movement play in their lives? How do they think and relate to their body? To food? Do they meditate or spend time in nature? How do they manage their stress and maintain a calm demeanor? What other behaviors might be important?

Make a list of qualities that will be essential for you to be this new you. Then choose three or four key characteristics and make it a priority to display them at every opportunity. Some of the qualities may be new for you; others you may already express.

Be vigorously honest with yourself. If you are not ready to proceed, it is better to be honest about it than lie to yourself and get stuck wishing things were different. Sometimes, we need help to be honest with and about ourselves. This is another place where a coach can be of great assistance. If you have a trusted friend, that person may be able to provide the objective insight needed.

Whenever we elevate something in importance, it grows. By focusing on developing your character, you advance emotionally and grow in maturity. You change! And you feel good about the change because this new you is healthier and happier and more empowered. You have expanded your capacity and have unleashed your potential. That's exciting stuff!

Develop Character

It is up to each of us to improve ourselves and "be all we can be." Society's focus on "doing" and "having" does not bring happiness; rather, you chase after something you think you are supposed to have, but even if you get it, you are still left feeling unfulfilled.

Character building involves becoming confident, dependable, and trustworthy. Focusing on this fulfills you. You are less needy when you live your life in integrity and with honor. If you are filled with a sense of lack, then no amount of chasing will fulfill you. You will only be satisfied when you build a stronger sense of self.

There are times when our lives are impacted by outside forces. The one thing you always have control over is you. Regardless of the events going on around you, ask yourself what you can do to improve your situation. What is here for you to learn? What is being asked of you now? In what ways might you be holding on to old habits and ideas? What are you attached to that is no longer serving you or adding value to your life? What might be some opportunities you can create from this situation?

Character development is becoming quite a big focus in education. There seems to be a gap in what our children learn in school and their ability to achieve success. A look at the level of violence in our schools speaks volumes about the character of our youth and the values that are being instilled.

Having an education in values, ethics, morals, empathy, respect, and even emotional competence will help us move forward as a society. Politicians often campaign on the return to family values, but do we even know what those are anymore? Have you ever stopped to consider what is of greatest value to you? And, once you identify these values, do you live them? Do you treat your family with the respect and loving-kindness that you profess? Do you treat yourself lovingly and respectfully?

Character development is about learning to "be the change you wish to see," as Mahatma Gandhi taught us. It is about who you are *being* as you go about *doing*. We are, after all, human *beings*—not human *doings*. By focusing on identifying and developing the qualities for being different, you become different. You grow and change how you think and what is important to you, then start to do different things. With this inside-out approach, *you* will change before your external world catches up to reflect the changes you have made in you. You become the kind of person who enjoys what you desire as a natural outcome and, eventually, your vision becomes reality.

Developing character is about defining what qualities are required and then living them each day. You grow and evolve as you take responsibility for your actions and make better choices. Accepting responsibility for yourself, your life, and the choices you make is the first step on the journey toward personal development. Without accepting responsibility, you live under the belief that others are responsible, you are a victim of circumstances, and outside forces or fate are to blame for your lot in life. With this mentality, you are powerless to change. You give your power away to these unseen forces!

Take your power back by accepting and embracing that you are capable and responsible for the quality of your life. Your results reflect your choices and values. Make better choices and you will enjoy better results. Build a better you and you will enjoy a happier life.

In my book, *The Journey Called YOU*, I provide a roadmap to accept and respect yourself and learn the ways of personal power. Learning to know yourself and make choices that honor who you are and who you want to become is the path to developing your confidence and creating a life you are proud of. It begins with moving along your personal development continuum and developing your character.

Update Your Self-Image

Your self-image is a snapshot of who you were; it is not the same as the person you want to be. You will need to update how you see yourself and how you refer to yourself in order to assist you in making the change permanent.

An outdated self-image is one of the barriers to achieving success. Being attached to seeing yourself a certain way keeps you from moving forward and embracing life as you change and grow.

Other people may also be attached to seeing you in a certain way. In their mind, they have a vision of you, an idea, and a description of who you are. If asked, they might give several adjectives to describe how they see you.

This can also get in your way and present an obstacle for change. As you decide to become someone new, other people may struggle with the changes you want to make. If you always went out to eat lunch with a friend and one day you decide to save your money or eat differently, you may want to do something new with that friend. They may not like this; they may question your decision and try to get you to keep things the way they are. If you were always a gossip and spoke about people negatively and have decided now you want to be seen as promotable and be more respectful of others, this change may not appeal to your gossip buddies or those who enjoyed partaking in the drama.

Others have their own resistance to change and may push that resistance onto you.

Change requires us to grow and develop ourselves, and in so doing, our relationships with others may change as well. This shows up when you are promoted to lead people who used to be your peers. Your relationship with them must change in order for them to accept you in this new role. You will also need to see yourself differently. A client remarked how she found it difficult to give directions or provide feedback to people who used to be her peers. She still saw them as her peers, yet she now had a different role, which meant there were different responsibilities and her staff needed something different from her. Before, she was not responsible for the results of the team, and now she is. She needed to learn to accept this new responsibility and espouse the qualities of a team leader rather than a peer.

Updating who you are and the image you see of yourself will take some time and courage. Some people in your life may not be supportive because they do not want you to change, or they may not wish to change themselves. Self-esteem is fragile. If you embark upon a change, instead of thinking of you and being happy for you, other people may think about themselves and how your change relates to them. They feel obligated to change themselves and feel pressured even though your change has nothing to do with them. This is one reason it is important to have the right support to assist you in making the changes you wish to make. We'll talk more about this in chapter 10 when I introduce strategy 4 on creating an environment to support the change.

Because people think of themselves and often compare themselves to others, they immediately put themselves into your situation and think of "me, me, me" rather than you. Even if they are happy for you, they often leave feeling sad for themselves that they are not in a position to change; they are not yet ready. Change requires courage to move forward in spite of what others think, feel, or do.

You are only responsible for you. As you grow and change and develop, you become a role model for others who wish to take the same path. The changes you make may inspire others to consider making their own change. You can be a resource; you can show them the way you traveled, but you cannot take them with you. People have to want to change for themselves. They have to be internally motivated and committed to doing whatever it takes.

Don't let your self-image be wrapped up in what other people think. And don't maintain an old self-image. Be willing to let go and see yourself anew. Look to your vision to update your self-image. How do you want to describe yourself? How do you want others to describe you?

Let your self-image change as you do. Revisit it frequently so that you do not hold on to old "snapshots" of you but rather embrace the amazing person you are developing into.

Develop Confidence

Your self-esteem, like your self-image, is created by thoughts. It is a habit of thought, how you think about you. You see yourself a certain way. You value yourself in a certain way.

Self-esteem can get in your way to success. The more you think about you and obsess over what you do, who you are, and how other people judge you, the less time you have to do what needs to be done. You are self-obsessed and have little personal "random access memory" (RAM) to think about other things, including other people.

When you have poor self-esteem, it shows up in many ways. You may spend time, energy, and effort focusing on pleasing others. This can prevent you from making a change out of fear that other people won't approve. You may do everything you can to impress others, in which case you may change only to get attention from others. While this may work to motivate you initially, it won't be enough to sustain the change. You are giving away your power.

Become the change you wish to see. Envision yourself as confident and self-assured. Consider what that feels like. Practice and nurture this feeling. Confidence grows as you develop your character, take action steps, and achieve success. Confidence is a character trait. It is attractive. We are magnetized by people who exude confidence and self-assurance.

Confidence is the belief you have in your ability to do what you set out to do. As you do the things you need to do through your commitment to change and follow these eight simple strategies for success, you begin to take action. You make progress along the way, and your wall starts to come down. You start to see how powerful you can be. You begin to believe change is possible. You believe in you, and you tell yourself a new story. This changes your inner environment to become much more encouraging, positive, and nurturing.

For now, put your self-esteem on a shelf and just do what you need to do. Don't concern yourself with what you think of you. It's judgment. It is an idea you have about who you were, not who you are, who you are capable of being, or who you are becoming.

Build Your Dependability Muscles

Becoming someone you can depend upon is important in the quest for change. When you become the kind of person who is dependable, then you trust yourself to do what you say you will do, and you develop your self-esteem. As you take little steps (strategy 5) and celebrate your successes (strategy 6), you begin to believe in yourself again—or for the first time. You learn over time that you can trust yourself, that you will stand up for yourself, and that you will follow through. (Believing you can succeed is strategy 8.)

If you cannot trust yourself, how can you expect to succeed? If you don't believe in yourself and have the confidence to perform, you are less likely to take the action steps required. You don't trust yourself to do what you need to do. This, then, becomes an act of self-sabotage. You resist out of the fear you project from past experiences; you won't finish or follow through because you have not done so in the past.

Dependability is an essential element in character development. It encompasses respecting yourself, following through, and exuding confidence. When you focus on getting the job done, there is less effort wasted on worry, resistance, and fear. You are too busy focusing on what needs to be accomplished and how you can take action.

There are three parts to building dependability:

1. Choose your words carefully.
2. Make a commitment.
3. Follow through.

What does dependability mean to you? How does it feel when someone does not return your call or email in a timely manner? What happens when someone tells you they'll do something, and they fail to deliver? Can you depend upon yourself to deliver? Let's explore each of these three elements to build dependability.

Choose your words carefully

To be credible and become someone who people (and you) can depend upon to get things done, take your word seriously. What you say matters. This means that when you say something, you mean it. You honor your word.

People say all sorts of things without meaning any of it. How often do we hear "Let's do lunch"? Whenever someone says this to me, I pull out my calendar (if it is someone I want to make time for). Sometimes, if the person doesn't know me well, they look at me funny. They are not used to having someone hold them accountable on their word.

If you don't mean it, don't say it.

Keeping your word is how you become reliable. It means doing what you say you will do. This is how we build trust in our relationships.

In his book *The Four Agreements*, Don Miguel Ruiz discusses the notion of "being your word." This is the congruency of who you are and what you do; it is how you are being. Being your word is rooted in integrity, while keeping your word is rooted in honesty and commitment. Keeping your word requires conscious effort, whereas being your word is your essence—it's who you are at your core and requires no effort. Keeping your word will pave the way for being your word. Both of these are extremely attractive.

Before committing to something new, make sure you are willing, able, and want to do the necessary work or have the required resources to complete the goal. If you don't want to do it, if you don't think the time is right given your other responsibilities, then say no. Learning to say no increases your self-esteem, gives you more energy, decreases your stress, allows you to complete your other commitments, and frees up time for more enjoyable things. It is respectful—to both you and the other person. It helps build trust in your relationships as people learn you are a person of your word. It also helps you to begin to trust yourself again. Learning to say no is not selfish; it's a requirement for effective life management and maximum enjoyment.

It is also essential in the quest for change. You may need to say no to things that you previously enjoyed. If they no longer fit into your vision for success, if they no longer add value, then they have outgrown their usefulness. Accept and embrace your current reality and let go of what was.

The words you choose make a difference in your believability. For example, pay attention to the use of the word "try." To *try* is not to *do*. If you were to ask someone over for lunch and they said they would try to come, would you cook? "Try" is a noncommittal word. It means that you have not yet made a decision. So, make a decision. What options do you have? Which choice makes you happier? Which choice are you willing to commit to?

If you're not yet ready to choose, then say that. Say you're not sure, that you haven't yet made a decision. Tell the truth, and that will add to your credibility.

Make a commitment

Make a commitment to yourself to do what you say you will do. This means taking your word seriously and committing to what you say. Commitment is an important character trait. If you agree to do something, do it, or don't agree to it.

Become more aware of what you say to yourself and others through the course of the day. Learning to say less is the precursor for honoring your word. It's much easier to honor your word when you've thought carefully about what you are promising! By promising less, it's more likely you'll be able to deliver. Each time you deliver what you say, you become more credible, and your words become more meaningful.

This aids you in developing the character for this new change you are making. You commit to an action, and when you take it, it feels good. You feel proud of yourself. This adds up over time. You develop your dependability muscle and begin to trust yourself. Others will trust you too.

If you are responsible to do something or complete something, then do it. You'll be glad when it's over. If there is something that stands in your way, move it, or arrange to have someone else do it. Don't let anything or anyone deter you from becoming a person of your word. Become a person whom others can depend upon and whom you can depend upon. Dependability means you are credible and trustworthy, and that people can place confidence in you and what you say. It takes time, courage, and repetition to develop. Each day offers new opportunities to practice.

If you truly cannot follow through on a commitment, take responsibility for it by letting the other people know. By taking your word seriously, you will find that you are more confident and that your self-respect increases, as does the respect you receive from others.

Follow through

Following through is the most important element of dependability. It means making a commitment and finishing things once they have begun. There is a glorious feeling one experiences when a project is completed, and it is important to celebrate your accomplishments (this is strategy 6). Having unfinished projects is both stressful and energy depleting. David Allen, the guru of time management and author of *Getting Things Done: The Art of Stress-Free Productivity*, states that one of the biggest sources of stress is not finishing what has been started. It behooves us to be careful in what we start in the first place.

There are several reasons why people don't follow through: procrastination, perfectionism, being overextended, being unable to say no, self-sabotage, and becoming discouraged. Pick your poison. What stands in your way?

On your quest for change, take care in what you choose to do so that whatever you agree to, you can complete it in a reasonable timeframe. By saying no to things that do not add value to your new path, you give yourself the gift of space in your time to be able to add things that are of value and that will move you toward your goals.

Sabotaging Your Success

There are many ways in which we can create obstacles that interfere with our success. Overcommitting is one way to sabotage your success. When you have too much to do and are not clear about your priorities, you are apt to flounder, become discouraged, and give up. This has been one of my personal struggles: having too many priorities and accepting too many projects to manage. In some ways, I do this to myself by taking on projects that could go to others or by creating unreasonable deadlines. This makes me stay busy and makes me feel important. However, I do not feel peaceful and calm. When life is busy, it feels hectic and rushed. And I feel stressed!

In what ways do you sabotage your success? Below are several self-sabotaging behaviors I've noticed in myself and others. Can you relate to any of these? What else might you be doing to hold yourself back?

- You make excuses, entertain discouraging thoughts, and begin to slow your progress.
- You forget about your commitment or why this is important to you.
- You neglect to nurture your vision.
- You stop noticing, acknowledging, and celebrating your success.
- You only see the long road ahead and not how far you have come.
- You question your ability and doubt yourself.
- You give up too soon.
- You stop having fun but rather think of how it used to be or how much better it will be when . . .

You succumb to these pervasive and cunning thoughts and turn back. Before you know it, you've returned to your old habits and recreated the past. You've regained the weight you had worked so hard to lose. You're back in debt again. You have stopped delegating and have too much on your plate. Oh no! How did this happen?

You forgot to pay attention. You forgot what you were working toward, and you neglected to develop the characteristics required to support your new life.

Self-sabotage is sneaky. Look for ways in which you trick yourself or put yourself in situations that could only lead to failure. For example, an addict will need to stay away from people who are actively using substances. An alcoholic will need to stay away from parties and places where liquor is being served, at least until he trusts himself to feel comfortable around it without using it (if ever). Someone who is working toward being debt-free will need to eliminate sources of credit such as credit cards and open lines of credit. Put up some roadblocks so it takes effort to go backward. Make it harder, if not impossible, for you to go back to where you've been.

Sometimes you must look for unconventional ways to develop your skills before you are ready for something bigger. For example, if you are seeking a promotion and keep getting passed over, then find other ways to develop your leadership skills. Get involved in an association by leading a committee or getting on the board, take the lead on a project, or ask for a stretch assignment. Find ways to break through the ceiling to your success. By pushing yourself, you will uncover the development area that needs attending, so you are prepared for that next position.

This is one reason to tell others about your goals. Talk to people about what you are working on. Tell others about your vision for success. In this way, you create external support to help you while you develop the skills and strength of character. Hiring a coach or other support professional is one way to ensure that you stay on track and hold yourself accountable for the changes you wish to make. It is an action step in the direction of your goal.

Character development sustains you. When you focus on developing the attributes of the kind of person you want to become, you begin to behave differently, and you grow internally. You are less likely to self-sabotage without realizing what you are doing because you are more aware, and the behaviors are out of alignment with the new characteristics you are striving to adopt.

If you choose not to proceed with your change, do so because it is what you want; do so because you have consciously decided you want to pursue another path. Don't just sabotage yourself and let success slip through your fingers. That's not being responsible, and it's not honorable or respectful of you.

A Test of Commitment

You may wonder why I have not discussed the concept of willpower. It is often said that if you cannot change your behavior, well, then you just don't have enough willpower. This implies there is some other force in charge over you—other than you. That is simply not true.

Willpower is hard; it has to do with forcing yourself to behave a certain way. We are on a quest for easy, so pushing yourself to behave in a certain way all the time is not an option; sometimes, maybe, but not all the time. And, let's face it, after all the decisions we have to make on any given day, we get tired, and any willpower we might have had earlier in the day disappears as the day progresses. This is known as decision fatigue.

Either you are committed or not. You will be tested for sure. You can limit your exposure to temptation, but there will be times when you cannot avoid being in front of the very thing you are working to change. The question is: What choice will you make? Will you choose to give in to temptation? Or will you stand firm in your commitment to your goal?

No one and nothing have to shake you from your goal! Consider the consequences of your actions. If you were to cheat on your diet and eat a donut, how would you feel? Guilty? Perhaps. Disappointed? For sure. Angry at yourself? Maybe.

How easy will it be to forgive yourself? Can you let it go? How important is it to you? Does this choice reflect the attributes of the kind of person you are working to become? Does it add value or not? Will you succumb to discouragement, or will you forgive and keep taking another step toward your goal? The reality is that you may fail many times before you achieve the success you desire. How will you handle the failure?

We all have setbacks in reaching a new goal. That does not mean you give up on your goal. You persist until you succeed. Focus on strengthening your commitment and resolve. Eventually, it will be easy to make choices that align with the new person you are becoming.

Sometimes, you may find that taking a bite of something unhealthy or fattening would be okay. You are celebrating a birthday or some other special occasion. Go for it! Do what you want to do and come from a place of choice. This is where your power is. Don't do it because you are giving in to the little voice in your head that wants you to fail or is waiting for you to falter so it can beat you up and torture you for the next week. Don't sabotage yourself.

Addicts, however, can never give in; it is all or nothing. They have an affliction, an allergy of sorts where "one is too many and a thousand is never enough." In other words, an addict might buy a dozen donuts and eat them all in one sitting. There is no off switch.

What are you committed to? If you are committed to your vision and you are clear about why this is important, then it should be fairly easy to know what the right choice is for you.

What would be of greatest value to you in this moment? The answer to this question might look different at different times. If you are famished and all that's available to eat is something you normally wouldn't, make the best choice you can. Forgive yourself and move on.

What are the attributes or qualities you want to adopt? Does this choice support those qualities? Once you identify the kind of person you want to become and the attributes that kind of person would display, then go out into the world and practice living them. These are not habits yet, so you cannot operate on autopilot. You cannot trust yourself yet. You must be on alert for these opportunities to practice and make a conscious choice, like saying no to a donut.

How Will Your Roles Change?

In the new landscape you are creating, how will your roles change? If you are a parent, for instance, and you are looking for love, how will adding a life partner change things for your children, whether they are adult children or still dependent? How might things change in your relationship with you and your ex-partner/spouse?

Changes we make impact others in our life, especially big changes. If you want to become a vegetarian, improve your health, or change your eating habits, how might this impact your family or friends? What will change in your relationship with food and with your body? What is the role health will play in your life that may be different from how it has been in the past?

Thinking these things through helps you to envision how you'll handle the change in your relationships. In this way, you can prepare others so they can adjust to the changes you are making for yourself.

For instance, if you have been sick for a long time, you may have formed a community with your family and others to cater to you and your physical needs. Your illness has played a role in the lives of those around you. As you heal and become healthy, the roles change and your needs change. You don't need the same charity and attention; you are now able to give to others who have needs. With less time spent traveling to doctors' offices and treatment centers, you will have more time to do more for yourself and to spend time playing or being with family and friends. There are many changes in this type of situation.

Smokers who become nonsmokers find themselves with more discretionary income. They will need to plan for how they will use that money to add value to their lives. The same is true for people who become debt free. As you pay off your bills, there will be money available for other uses. Plan ahead what you will do with it; be intentional about its use. Anticipate these extra funds and save them or use them wisely.

In addition, as you become debt free or increase your wealth, money will have a different meaning, and your role will change as a consumer and as a saver. Your relationship with debt, shopping malls, and banking institutions will change. Instead of being a debtor, for instance, you will become an investor. Your banker will treat you differently, and you will share a different relationship with your finances as well as the people with whom you associate to handle your finances, including your accountant and financial advisor. Instead of going to the mall to window shop, you may choose to go to stores only when there is a need to do so, and you go with a budget and cash—no credit card. You find other ways to spend your time that bring you joy and fulfillment.

As you move up in the hierarchy at work, your role changes, and the relationships you have with others change. You may become a boss to someone you were once friends with, or a friend may have been promoted and now you report to them. People you used to look up to now become peers. Instead of looking up to them, now they are learning from you and following your lead.

Changes in roles occur throughout our lives. As we grow up, for instance, the relationship that we have with our parents changes. As we embrace adulthood and are responsible for our lives and choices, we no longer need our parents in the same way we did when we were young. Our roles need to be reevaluated so that we can adjust the relationship to enjoy our parents differently than when we needed them to care for us. What kind of relationship would you like to have with each of your parents? What might they now need from you? What is the role that you would like to play in their lives now that you are grown? If you are the parent, what is the role you will play in your adult child's life? How will that relationship morph now that they do not need you in the same way?

Look beyond yourself as you start to change so you can anticipate the rippling effects to others. Roles will change. Relationships will change. It's all good. It's a reflection of healthy transitions. You will grow, and so will those whom you connect with along the way. All of this adds to the sustainability of the change. Your self-image changes, and the image others have of you changes. You become the change you wish to see.

Easy.

CHAPTER 10

STRATEGY 4: CREATE AN ENVIRONMENT TO SUPPORT THE CHANGE

"We begin to see, therefore, the importance of selecting our environment with the greatest of care, because environment is the mental feeding ground out of which the food that goes into our minds is extracted."

—Napoleon Hill

Get the Right Support Systems in Place

As you develop your inner environment, you will also need to create an external environment to help nurture the changes you wish to make. You need a group of supportive people as well as structure and support from your surroundings. In this way, you ensure your success.

If you want to change who you are, spend time with people who exhibit the qualities you want to aspire to: be around them, learn from them, develop those qualities, become the kind of person who would have the results you seek.

There will be people who are beginning the process just like you. There will be those who have more experience whom you can learn from. And then, after a while, there will be newbies who can learn from you. You become a mentor to others.

Left to your own thoughts—those fifty thousand repetitive, obsessive thoughts that are attached to being right and having their way—you are apt to flounder, get frustrated, and lose your way. There is a saying in addiction treatment programs, "Don't go upstairs without adult supervision." The mind can be a messy place, and we can get lost in our thoughts, beliefs, and stories if we cannot separate ourselves from them and see them for what they really are—just thoughts, ideas, and stories that we have made up.

You need others around to help you question your old beliefs and habits of thought. Others can help you stay focused, motivated, and encouraged, teach you what you do not know, and, most importantly, keep you from those self-sabotaging behaviors. They can only help you, however, if you are willing and open to receive the information and feedback, to listen when they reflect back behaviors they see or stories they hear you cling to. There are strong factors working to keep you the same—habits, attachment to ideas, resistance, fear, denial, and discouragement—these can be quite tricky, as you know.

You also want to set up the space around you to support your success, to assist you in creating the future you envision. Before dieting, for example, it is recommended that you clean out your pantry of all junk food and items that you will no longer be eating. If it isn't there, you are less likely to indulge. Or at the very least, you would have to go to some trouble to obtain the food you are craving.

Someone who is working toward freedom from debt may cut up credit cards and perhaps hire a credit counseling or arbitration company to assist them to follow through and take the steps required to eliminate their debt. Depending upon how much debt and the amount payable monthly, eliminating debt may take several years to accomplish. Having the right support and a simple structure in place will help you persevere until completion.

At work, it is helpful to have a mentor, if you can find one, or work with your boss, if they are able and interested in supporting your development. Many workplaces have career paths; they may provide access to coaches or offer leadership development courses, which can be helpful in providing not only information and education but also a supportive community for helping you in your development goals. If you do not have that support system at work, then look for an association, external coach or peer coach, or other resource outside of your workplace to help support you with your goals.

Because initially, all you have is your vision and your commitment (along with your old habits and attachments), the appropriate external environment is essential to help you stay on track and gain the momentum you need to go the distance.

In your future vision, your environment looks different than it is today. There are things—equipment, people, processes, and structures—that you don't have today but which are present in your future. Start identifying those supports now and putting them into place. While there may be things that you need to prepare and to support you in order to get started, such as cleaning out your pantry, along the way, you will also be creating an environment that suits your new life as part of the process of change.

It is rare that you can do it all yourself. There are many forces at work to throw you off track and sabotage your success—inside your mind and in your current external environment:

- Your environment is arranged to maintain the status quo. It is comfortable and familiar.
- Your habits are ingrained.
- You're attached to your old ways, your ideas, and your stories.
- You have sentimental feelings about certain things that you hate to let go of.

- You have excuses and attachments.
- You have resistance and fear.
- You get discouraged.

As you embark upon change, everything gets uprooted. Shaping your external environment and having the right support is a key strategy for solidifying your commitment and for going the distance.

Meet Your Wall

Thinking you can do it all yourself is a trap. It is resistance. You are hiding behind a wall of mistrust and fear.

There's something about having the answer, having it all together, or being "right" that keeps you from reaching out to others. Inevitably, by swimming in your own thoughts and without new information or new perspectives, you can get lost.

Perhaps your pride gets in the way of reaching out for assistance. There are thought processes that, if left unattended, will "should you" to death—you *should* know, you *should* have figured it out, and you certainly *should not* have to ask someone else for assistance.

You want to be right, and if you ask others for help, you interpret this to mean you are wrong. That is a hard pill to swallow.

Then there is your fear—fear of what others will think of you, fear of being vulnerable, fear of being wrong, fear of being judged, fear of being rejected or humiliated, fear of being stuck and unable to find a solution . . .

It's frustrating, disappointing, and aggravating when you come to the realization that, in this situation, you don't know which way to turn, and your regular method of operating isn't working. You don't (yet) know how to achieve a positive result.

You are now a beginner. It is not wrong or bad. It can be scary to embark on a new path. There is a story you tell yourself about being in this place. What are your beliefs about embarking upon a new path, something untried? How might you let go of the story, of needing to be right, and embrace a beginner's mind? Instead of thinking of this as a problem, how might you approach it as a new adventure?

You are not alone. There are many other people with the same struggles going through the same issues. There are people embarking on the same path and who may be at different places on the path you are now seeking to travel. Do not compare yourself to others and then judge yourself against them. Each person is on their own journey. Those who have advanced are often very willing to give and provide support and teach. Everyone has their own fears—and their own walls of doubt, suspicion, fear, and resistance. We can learn from each other and help each other to bridge those walls—if we dare. We have to be more committed to doing whatever it takes than we are to maintaining our wall.

People want to make a difference in the lives of others. They want to feel needed and valued and included. They are looking for students who they can teach. They want the opportunity to get to know you— your thoughts, ideas, feelings, fears, and doubts. They want to share their knowledge and struggles and learn what they can from you as well. We all want to be known.

Let others in by sharing yourself with others whom you feel comfortable and safe around. Take a chance. You'll find that it takes strength and courage to open up and be vulnerable, and there is so much to be gained when you do. It's extremely liberating when you don't have to hold back on being you—when you can live without your wall. It's easier when you can just do you and express yourself authentically without shrinking or holding back or living behind the wall of fear and doubt. And change is so much easier when you don't have to do it all by yourself, when you can learn from and share your journey with others.

Asking for help from the right support system is essential. In an attempt at being helpful, people around you—such as friends, colleagues, even your spouse—will gladly tell you what you should do or what they would do in your situation. People like to share their opinions about everything. It's always interesting, for instance, to listen to people complain about management when they have never been a manager or talk about how to raise children when they have none of their own, or when an overweight medical provider gives you nutrition advice. It can be a challenge to take them seriously.

When you join a community or even a small group of like-minded people who share the same goal or who are working on the same challenges, you know they understand. They have been where you are, and you can easily relate to each other.

Sometimes, you do have the answer, but you just cannot access it through all of the other thoughts in your mind. You're not clear. You are stuck in your own mind muck. The muck gets in your way from seeing the right path, and you would benefit greatly from someone who can elicit from you your own best thinking. Coaches are trained in the art of asking questions to do just that—help you to explore your thinking and beliefs.

For you to enjoy and appreciate the support of others, however, you need to be open to new perspectives and ideas. You need to be willing to listen and to explore new possibilities. This does not mean you have to follow everything the person says; you take what works for you and throw out the rest. But you need to be open. You need to break through the attachments and any need to be right you may be harboring. This can be a barrier to change. It can show up as an inability to listen to the ideas of others, being very judgmental, and finding fault with or pushing back on anything that differs from your view. If you cannot be wrong, how likely is it that you would be willing to ask someone for assistance? If you think you know it all, you will struggle to hear new ideas; even if you ask for help, you aren't really interested or willing to hear what is being shared. You will not be open to change. It's as if you are fighting against the very thing you want.

This is your wall.

Notice it. Often when people struggle to ask for help, they have issues with trust or self-esteem. Their fear brings their attention to issues related to old wounds. There is unresolved pain.

This is good! It is always good to discover a piece of your wall because then you can do something about it. You don't have to hide behind it anymore or live as if it is the truth. You now have a choice, and that is powerful!

Often, when trust is damaged, you build a wall to protect you from future pain. You don't realize you are doing this at the time. Although this wall serves a purpose, it also keeps you from enjoying people. While you remain safely behind your wall keeping people out, the wall also keeps you in. The best of you is hiding behind the wall. This impacts your relationships and your ability to connect deeply with others.

You can certainly revisit your past to determine where trust was lost (just don't get lost there!). In this way, you can feel the pain, learn why the wall was built, and then, you can choose to bring down the wall. You no longer need that wall to keep you safe. You have grown and are not the same person you were then. You can make better choices. You are doing what you need to do today to build trust in yourself, and by respecting yourself, you rebuild self-trust. The fear you feel about being hurt again relates to the past being projected into the future. You expect to be hurt again. By having these thoughts echo in the background of your mind, you recreate this in your reality. You behave in ways that will fulfill this forecast or expectation. To stop the pattern, change the expectation. Change the story.

Look at all of the people in your life who *are* trustworthy: professors, colleagues, family members, clergy, friends, neighbors. If you cannot think of anyone in your life today that you can trust, then hire someone. Find a coach or counselor with the qualities and attributes you want to emulate and hire them to teach you. You are committed to your success! You will do whatever it takes! This is a hurdle you must overcome. It is keeping you from achieving the very thing you want—to enjoy and experience deep connections and happiness and love.

Learn to trust again—or for the first time. Trusting yourself has a lot to do with it. When you trust yourself, you make better choices about who to trust. You attract people into your life who are trustworthy. You trust yourself to make better choices about people. You become more intuitive and trust your gut when it tells you there is something wrong. You also learn to be more assertive and to ask for what you need.

If you feel you have to do it yourself or that you are "less than" if you ask for help, then your self-esteem may be tied to your ideas. There are ingrained thought processes creating a wall of resistance that is sabotaging your success and keeping you distant from others. These thoughts are not serving you.

We are not supposed to know it all or figure it all out by ourselves. There is tremendous value in hearing other people's perspectives. We are social beings, and we need each other to learn from and to teach and to collaborate. We are at our best when we can live in our own genius, teach others from our expertise, and learn from theirs.

In order to do this, we must learn to bring down our wall to expose the best of ourselves and help others to do the same.

Don't be afraid to ask for the assistance you need. You may have the answer but are simply lost in the abyss of your own thoughts and need someone to guide you safely to shore. Or perhaps you need new thoughts or new information. Either way, if you leave yourself with only your own thoughts, you could be sabotaging your own happiness and success.

People, Places, and Things

In addiction treatment programs, there is a lot of discussion about people, places, and things because it is not just the addicted substance that the person needs to let go of; everything they associate with it needs to be let go of as well.

In other words, you cannot visit the bar you used to frequent on a regular basis if you are no longer drinking alcohol. It's not just the bar that is the problem but also the people, conversations, and things you associate with the bar, such as playing darts or pool. For an alcoholic, this is trouble. The only reason to enter this environment is to torture oneself or to fail. With repeated exposure to the very thing they are trying to give up, eventually, the alcoholic will give in to his addiction and will use alcohol again.

There is a whole host of things that you associate with the status quo that will need to change in addition to the specific change you wish to make. It's never just one thing. For the overeater, it's the preparation of the food, the purchasing of the food, the emotions they feel around food and their body, and any associations they make with food.

This doesn't mean that an overeater can never have dessert, or the alcoholic can never visit an establishment that serves alcohol; but it may take the alcoholic years to feel comfortable and safe entering that environment again. An overeater may find it best to give up refined sugars altogether. Given the statistics, an alcoholic will never be able to drink again successfully.

The same is true for parties or family members who are drinkers. People with whom you associate your addiction need to be left behind or kept at a distance while you heal, change, and gain strength. There is no way of knowing how long it will take you to return to these environments—if you can return at all.

There is a dynamic to the way things were in your life. This dynamic needs to change. You will need to stop doing things the way you have always done them and start doing things differently. The old you must give way for a new you to be born.

Evaluate your current environment; ask yourself whether this person, place, or thing adds value and brings you closer to your vision for a new life. If you are not sure, then err on the side of caution, at least at first. Protect yourself while you gain momentum and strength.

When in doubt, do without.

Your environment is essential for your success. The things that helped you create the old you may not serve the new you. It is often difficult to accept that you will need to let go of certain people in your life. People may be in our lives only for a time or for a reason, and when that time is up or that purpose has been resolved, it may be time to move on. You love them, but they are not on the same path as you. This doesn't make them wrong; they are just on a different journey.

This was true of my first marriage. My first husband and I were together for both a time and a reason. We needed each other during that time of our lives. Eventually, we outgrew the reasons we came together, and it was time to go our separate ways. Each of us had grown and changed in different ways, and we needed different things that the other could no longer provide. We accepted this and were able to divorce amicably. We remained friends until his untimely death in 2002.

Other people, like family, will need new boundaries. The relationship, in other words, will need to be redefined and certain limitations or boundaries put in place to protect you. Roles may change. Eventually, the dynamic will adjust, but it will require consistent attention and vigilance to first change you and your approach, and then for the other person to adapt.

For example, if you are in a marriage that has become "convenient" without affection or passion, there are many things that will need to be worked through, such as the anger and resentment that have built up over the years. Once you consciously decide that you are committed to this relationship and want to change it for the better, you can start to change the dynamic by first stopping how you interact in ways that are damaging, and then looking for what is good about your partner and what you enjoy about your life together. Acknowledging what you like about each other will shift the negative energy to positive energy, and you will begin to appreciate one another and what you are able to share together.

Gratitude and appreciation have amazing healing powers. For this type of change, you may want to get support from a couples' therapist or relationship coach. There are different dynamics and behaviors in healthy, loving relationships than ones that have gone stale, and you will need to learn new ways of interacting to create a healthier partnership.

By starting to see the positive and acknowledging the other person, you begin to create an environment where the other person feels good. Boosting them up, rather than putting them down, begins the process of change. It will take time, mind you, for the trust to build and for the person to feel safe without fear of judgment or criticism, especially if the old dynamic has been going on for a long time. But with time and consistency, the walls that were built between you will start to come down, and you will once again be able to enter the other's heart. Then, you can start to do some real work to resolve the anger and create a new vision for your relationship—one that is grounded in respect and loving-kindness.

This would be true of a work relationship as well. Difficulties between colleagues can be shifted to create a respectful, professional relationship. These same steps for change would be required.

An environment—whether that environment is a relationship or a situation, such as a workplace—should provide a space that is safe, respectful, welcoming, and comfortable so that you can be your best self. It should allow you to be who you are and encourage you to be your best. When it feels bad or uncomfortable, where you walk on eggshells, where it is not safe to be yourself, then the friendship, relationship, situation, or workplace should be challenged. Is this adding value to you? Does this person or place enable you to be who you want to be? Are you able to change it so that it can be safer for your honest self-expression? If not, then you may need to consider how to adjust either with extending your boundaries or with changing the nature of the relationship, perhaps ending it, or finding new employment.

People, places, and things will change as you change and grow. Be willing to let go, remain unattached, and move on to be open to receive new and better things that are in store for you to enjoy. Initially, taking a step away and retreating from the things and the people you know may serve you until you get your bearings in your new you. Then you can consciously choose which people, places, and things are healthy for you to welcome into your new life and which need to be left behind.

Misery Loves Company

Everyone has their own fears and resistance behaviors. Fear is pervasive, but most people are unaware of the impact of their own fear. So they project their fears and their negative thoughts onto others. They mean no harm; they don't realize what they do.

If you embark upon a change, people may immediately and automatically think of themselves and how making this kind of change would impact them if they would change it in their lives. They get scared because they cannot conceive of making that kind of change. They are not ready and don't want that kind of change, so they tell you that you shouldn't want it either. "What do you want to do that for?"

When I began dating again, I ran into slighted women and men who were angry about their previous relationships. They were still carrying the pain of their past, and it was blinding them to the beauty and pleasure found in being in a loving and healthy relationship. I felt sad for them, but I was on a mission to help myself. I knew I wanted to create an amazing relationship, and I was committed to finding someone to share my life with. So I stayed away from these people. I did not hang out with these women when they would get together, and I did not date any man who was carrying that kind of baggage. I did not want to subject myself to negative energy. The Law of Attraction is quite clear that we must maintain our energy to attract what we want and *not* what we don't want.

This is another reason to be careful who you share your goals with. People may try to talk you out of it or to sabotage you in some way. They may not want you to change. They may be invested in your staying the same. A boss, for instance, may not want you to be promoted, because they would have to find a replacement. A colleague also may not want you to move to another department for fear that they would have to pick up your workload. A spouse may be fearful if you make more money than they do.

I have coached several clients over the years who have left their career to find something new. It can be scary to be out of work for a time, especially if you have no savings to cover your bills. In the cases of these clients, however, money was not the issue, and they wanted time to consider their options before jumping back into the workforce.

In every case, there were friends and family who had a very difficult time with the client not working. It was not about my clients' not working; people projected their own fears about being out of work onto my clients. This would feel very uncomfortable, and my clients would have to learn to manage this by either changing the subject or not discussing the job search strategies at all with these people. (That is what they hired me to do with them!)

This happens often where others project their pain or fears onto you. A child may not want you to find a new love after a divorce. They may have fantasies of you and their other parent getting back together. We often hear stories of children sabotaging the happiness of one parent because they cannot accept that the parent has moved on with a new love relationship.

People who know you are accustomed to knowing you in a certain way. They have their own ideas about who you are and what you should be doing with your life. There is an image of you they hold in their minds. If you change, that image then needs to change. People don't like change. Your changing, then, impacts them.

Don't let that stop you. Focus on doing what is best for you. You are not here living your life to make other people happy; you have to make yourself happy. Life, liberty, and the pursuit of happiness means *your* happiness, not striving to make other people happy. You do you. You define who you are and who you become. At the end of your life, you answer to yourself as to whether you lived your life well. Other people will come around. Perhaps watching you change and grow will be the impetus they need to create change for themselves. Or they won't accept that you have changed, and you will need to move on.

All of us know someone who is a naysayer. It is that person who tells you that you can't do it or that it cannot be done. Naysayers will tell you every way you could fail in your attempt to change. Some people are very positive and can be overly optimistic, never seeing the problems that could occur. Other people are negative and see only risk. They have difficulty seeing the possibility. For me, I tend to be very optimistic, always seeing the good and the possibilities. Which are you?

If you can manage it without becoming angry or emotional, take a moment to listen to the naysayer. Ask them a question about their ideas and be curious about what they have to say. Although negative, there can be value and usefulness to their thinking. You might hear some things that you should be aware of in your quest to change. For example, if you tend to jump into things without thinking things through or are overly optimistic, the naysayer may help you to be more realistic in your expectations. They will inform you of everything that could possibly go wrong, giving you great insight so you can avoid risk. With this information, you can then plan accordingly.

For me, my father played this role in my life. When I was young, I did not appreciate his perspective. He is very cautious and risk adverse. I viewed his comments as pessimistic and deterring, even controlling. I often fell into the trap of getting defensive and dug my heels into my ideas even further. I did not want to be told what to do or discouraged from my plans! (Can you picture the two-year-old stomping her feet with her hands on her hips?) As I grew older (and wiser, perhaps), I considered his view of risk and caution as an opportunity to expand my understanding of the situation and identify potential pitfalls. I also came to understand that he wanted me to succeed and was worried for me and the choices I was making. While his ideas and viewpoints did not stop me from proceeding with my plans, they often provided me with a frame of reference I had not considered, which enabled me to make some adjustments and avoid unintended consequences.

Do not allow the naysayer to beat you into submission. Once you've heard them share their viewpoints, thank them and leave. Don't subject yourself to repeated tirades. This will only drain you and cause you to become discouraged. Don't let anything shake you from pursuing your goals.

Extend Your Boundaries Where Needed

There are naysayers who tend to talk a lot but who are essentially harmless, and then there are those who can actually sabotage you. They may try at every opportunity to derail your efforts. This is unacceptable and requires your attention and swift action, especially if you cannot easily disengage. They may be family or colleagues, even neighbors or long-time friends, people with whom there is a relationship where cutting ties is not a possibility.

People do not have to agree with or like the changes you make. You cannot control whether they support you or not. They do, however, need to respect your wishes for change. You may need to teach them appropriate ways to treat you within the context of your new you. In other words, define how the relationship may be different or if there are new rules within which to function. Inform others of these changes. They may not like these rules, and they may not agree. They have the right to refuse, at which point you may need to make decisions about the importance of the relationship. There are adult children who will not speak with their parents and parents who no longer speak with their children. The need to control can have a big impact on relationships.

Just as you have the right to change, and those changes may impact your relationship, the other person has the right to make choices they believe are in their best interest. They can be stubborn or difficult, they can choose to be respectful but unhappy about it, or they can respect your wishes without difficulty.

You have certain expectations of how others will behave. These expectations are defined as boundaries; they are the behaviors that people may or may not do in your presence.

People may not be aware of your boundaries. You may not realize your boundaries either, until someone crosses the line, and you feel bad about what has been done. You notice through your emotional response: Identify the feeling and its message and how it relates to the person's behavior. Then inform the person of the behavior that is unacceptable. You can simply say, "This doesn't work for me." Then you can go on to describe what doesn't work for you. Often, you can use a question to bring their attention to the unwanted behavior: "Do you realize you are raising your voice?" Sometimes you need to be more specific and descriptive: "We are not going to discuss my weight or my food choices."

Tell people what doesn't work for you and ask people for what you prefer instead. "Please lower your voice so that we can have this conversation. I am interested in what you have to say."

If people do not respect your wishes, have a plan in place for how you will handle it. They have the right to refuse. They are humans practicing free will. If they don't want to do as you have asked, you will still need to take care of yourself. People will, however, need to be informed of this new rule and that they are expected to follow it.

You may decide to become a vegetarian while your spouse continues to eat meat. You can change without your spouse needing to change too. The two of you need to discuss how you will work together so that both of you have your needs met. It is not appropriate to expect that your spouse should change just because you do. Your spouse is not wrong for their choices just as you are not wrong for yours. They can continue to eat as they desire while you create the changes you wish to make.

Be clear about exactly what you need from the different people in your life and be direct in your request for support. You may need to get different needs met by different people.

Stay clear of people who are not supportive. Create strong boundaries and a "tough skin" to protect you when you must spend time with them. One of my clients has a mother who is very controlling and can often be mean. My client spends a considerable amount of time with her mother. With each encounter, her self-esteem takes a beating, and she walks away questioning her sense of self and her right to make choices in her best interest. When this woman decided to become a vegetarian, her mother gave her quite a hard time.

While you may not want to eliminate certain people from your life, limit your exposure, brace yourself when you do interact with them, and put up a strong boundary about how they are permitted to speak with you. Create rules around which topics are off-limits if necessary. Prepare yourself for your interactions. Expect that they will treat you as you desire and respect you and your wishes. When they do not, call them on it—each and every time. It is not acceptable. Perhaps they just need more time to adjust.

Focus on respecting yourself. Do not let negative people knock you off course. You are committed to this change! This is *your* life! They do not have to agree or like what you do, but they do need to respect you.

Most importantly, *you* need to respect you.

Adopt a New Community

> *"Friendship is born at that moment when one person says to another: 'What! You, too? I thought I was the only one.'"*
>
> —*C. S. Lewis*

Having someone on your side to motivate and inspire you, to believe in you, to hold you accountable, and to make sure you follow through and stay on task can mean everything to your success. This is evidenced by the success of coaching as a profession. As a coach, I become a supportive environment for my clients. You can benefit greatly by working with someone who has your back, who acknowledges and celebrates your progress with you, who points out your blind spots, who cheers you on when you're on that last lap, and who encourages you when you are struggling to turn a corner. They pick you up when you fall, hug you when you're down, and hold you up when you are barely hanging on.

People who have been where you are now have much to teach you. You learn from their mistakes, so you don't have to repeat them. This decreases the time it takes to achieve your goal and eliminates unnecessary detours. You become motivated by their successes. You start to think, *Hey, if they can do it, I can do it too!* You begin to believe in the possibility that you, too, can succeed.

Together you celebrate your successes (this is strategy 6). Often, your improvements go unnoticed by you while others recognize how much you have progressed! And by sharing what they notice, they help you recognize it and acknowledge it too. This way, you see the progress rather than minimize it or blow it off as nothing.

There is no greater feeling than knowing you are not alone. Being surrounded by people who think like you and who are experiencing the same struggles, pain, and success is exhilarating. It's uplifting and exciting to have this kind of community support.

It's so easy today to find like-minded people too. With the internet and the many online communities available, you can easily tap into one.

Surrounding ourselves with people who are on the same journey helps to get us out of our own thinking, break through our resistance, and stay honest. We are less likely to lie to ourselves, set unrealistic expectations, or play games. Our community will challenge us to be better than that.

The thinking that got us here won't get us where we want to go. With a supportive community, we can watch others and learn from our observations. We can identify the attributes that lead to success and learn how to integrate them into our lives. We can also learn ways to integrate new behaviors and create new habits as well.

Your external environment helps to support the internal environment you are creating in order to sustain the change and become someone new. Surrounding yourself with others who are traveling the same journey makes it easier to change. You want to be like them! It also makes the journey much more enjoyable when it is shared with others who have a similar goal.

An Essential Element for Success

"I am a success today because I had a friend who believed in me, and I didn't have the heart to let him down . . ."

—*Abraham Lincoln*

The right support provides you with motivation, connection, and inspiration. They see your blind spots, teach you what you didn't know you needed to know, and offer new perspectives and possibilities. Having support also offers you accountability. You are more likely to follow through and live up to your word when others are cheering you on and looking forward to hearing about your progress.

You learn from the mistakes and the successes of others. People teach you what they have learned along their journey. You also discover the attributes and characteristics required to achieve the success you desire. As you observe others displaying these attributes, you learn ways to practice them in your life. You have to be prepared for success; having the right people on your side will help you learn what you need to know when you reach the finish line.

You are not alone. There are many others going through the same thing as you are, and they, too, are seeking someone with the same goals to work with them to achieve success. Some people find an accountability buddy helps them to stay on track. Someone is looking for you to support them! Don't hide behind your wall. You need others to help you stay out of your head and your old thoughts.

Often the things people share with you are things you already know. We all need reminders. We know how to give advice; it is harder to put that advice and best thinking into practice for ourselves. Having supportive and like-minded people around you to remind you of things you know but may not be practicing makes a huge difference.

It also feels really good to know that someone believes in you, especially when it is so easy for us to get discouraged and misplace the belief in ourselves.

Set up your environment so that the people closest to you support you as well. Your spouse can check in with you on your progress, as can your family and friends. Most people want you to succeed. They want the best for you, and if you make healthy changes, they will want to support and encourage you. Ask them to help you in this way.

In addition to support, changing your surroundings so that they nurture your success is essential. Look around at the things you own and the places you visit. Do they support you in your new life? Are there things and places you need to add? What things might need to be eliminated?

By creating an external environment and spending time with like-minded people, you encapsulate and buffer yourself from the forces that are trying so hard to keep you from succeeding. Your old Habits, Attachments, Resistance, and Discouragement can all be dealt with easier when you immerse yourself in an environment suited for your new life. This environment will nurture and foster the characteristics and behaviors you are learning. It will nourish you when you are struggling and celebrate with you when you achieve success.

Don't get too attached, however. Once you have advanced and grown, you may change yet again and leave behind this support system for a new one. Environments change as your needs change. People come into your life for a time and a reason. Create the environment and the support you need for today to get you where you want to go—let go of what was, set boundaries with people who are not supportive, and prepare yourself for what's to come. You are on your way to success!

CHAPTER 11

STRATEGY 5: TAKE ACTION

"The vision must be followed by the venture. It is not enough to stare up the steps—we must step up the stairs."

—Vance Havner

Without Action, Nothing Changes

Change asks much of you: to surrender, to let go of all you've known; to embark upon an unknown future—a vision you created in your mind; to let go of the past and leave your comfort zone for uncharted waters; to commit to this new journey so there is no turning back; and to acknowledge your feelings: anticipation, excitement, and fear.

Along the way, your mind plays tricks with you to sabotage you and throw you off course. You will do battle with your inner demons. Through the process, however, you will get to know your demons, and once exposed, you can learn ways to move beyond them and succeed. You will grow stronger than you have ever been and achieve more than you thought was possible.

Strategy 5 is about taking action. Without action, nothing changes. You can think about it, talk about it, plan for it, envision it, commit to it, and want it with every fiber of your being, but if you do not take one step to achieve your goal, you will never achieve success.

The First Step

> *"You don't have to see the whole staircase,*
> *just take the first step."*
>
> —*Martin Luther King Jr.*

Once you define the change you want to make, create a plan. Write it down. This becomes the map to your destination. What are the things you will need to do? What resources and support will you need? What knowledge or information do you need? What do you need to eliminate? Identify what you want and list the things you will need in order to get there. By thinking things through, you prepare yourself for the journey.

Some people create a timeline and then work backward. If you want to accomplish something in a particular time, let's say a year, where will you need to be as you approach that last month? What will you work on in the last month? What will you need to accomplish prior to that? And what needs to be prepared in order for you to be able to accomplish that? Keep working your way backward until you know how to begin and what needs to be accomplished first. You can also assess whether your timeline is realistic. Can this reasonably be completed within one year? Of course, you can always adjust your timeframe along the way.

Other people enjoy just getting started with minimal planning. Having an outline of sorts is enough to keep them focused and on track. A compelling vision will pull you forward, and once you are committed, the path becomes clear, and you know what you need to do. Continuing to visualize what's next, you are able to see the steps you need to take to achieve a certain level of success, and you set small goals for yourself. For many people, this is enough to help them stay focused and move forward.

There is no one way that works best; the best plan is the one that works for you. Without a specific goal and a plan, however, you are apt to flounder, forget where you are in the process, and get lost, or forget what you were working toward. It's like setting off for a trip to a new destination without directions or a map. You have the address (the goal) but no idea how you would get from here to there. Without instructions or a navigation device, you would wander around forever trying to find your way. The same is true for change.

Create a plan. Write it down. Prioritize so you know what comes first, what's second, and what comes after that. Prepare yourself for what you know will be coming. Follow the plan but be open and flexible to make adjustments, assess and evaluate your efforts, and adapt as necessary. Be committed to your vision and to doing the work. Don't become attached to the plan. It's just a plan; an idea. It's not truth, and you may not have the answers when you start out. You have to be open to new possibilities along the way.

Some people spend enormous amounts of time in the planning phase. Businesses do this. They can get so caught up in planning the "right way" that much time and resources are wasted creating these great plans when, in a matter of moments, a disaster could strike or some other external event could occur that would change everything: a key person in the company dies, takes ill, or leaves the company; the company is bought out; the economy changes; a competitor comes out with a new product that surpasses theirs. Any number of things can impact the success of your plan.

It's just a plan. Create one. Keep it simple. If it is too complicated, you won't do it. If it feels like a chore, you won't do it. Don't get stuck here. Just map out some of the steps you will need to take and then take the first step.

Take Baby Steps

You've finished writing out your plan or your simple outline, and, in reviewing it, you become completely overwhelmed. There is so much to do! It's going to take forever! You become overwhelmed because you think of the entire goal all at once and cannot imagine how you will make it to the finish line. You cannot see five years down the road or all the steps it will take for you to get from here to there. All you see is the mountain of debt or the long list of courses you must take to complete your degree. The goal is too big, and it takes too long.

Entertain these thoughts and you start to believe that success is not possible. You begin to feel discouragement and resistance rise within you. The good news is that you notice it. This is a good thing. Because of your increased self-awareness, you can take charge of it.

Take a deep breath.

How do you eat an elephant? One bite at a time.

How do you travel a journey of a thousand miles? One step at a time.

The key to success is to cut your goal into bite-size portions. With each piece a manageable size, you can take steps to complete it fairly easily and then celebrate your success. Each accomplishment then builds on another until you reach your destination. Right now, you are just getting going. You have to start your engine and put the car into drive. Eventually, you will pick up speed and gain momentum.

One step at a time. One mile at a time. One bite at a time.

Working on my dissertation for my doctorate was a massive project. This strategy really helped me. Each time I would sit down at the computer, I would spend six to eight hours researching and reading research articles, and at the end of my time, I would feel like I had nothing to show for the work since I had not written anything! But then, I would breathe, and take a look at what I did get done. I might have a stack of new articles to review, and a list of article references for the bibliography, and that small accomplishment was huge for getting this project completed. It was one (perhaps small) bite of the elephant, but a necessary bite to get me to the finish line.

Becoming overwhelmed is another way we sabotage ourselves. We overload our plate with responsibilities in a short timeframe, which makes us anxious as we attempt to get it all accomplished, and, in the process, we neglect our goals.

This is a trick your mind plays, causing you to resist change. There is no time to focus on your goal, no time to plan, and no time to make changes. Feeling overwhelmed signifies that you need to simplify and do less. Remember, one step at a time, one bite at a time. When there is too much stimulation, you can become anxious. This feeling then causes adrenaline to be released, and your stress response is triggered. You either freeze and do nothing or become stressed out trying frantically to get it all done.

Notice the feeling of overwhelm and breathe. It is only an emotion bringing you a message, and the message is that you are trying to do too much at once. Don't judge it, accept that it is too much, and choose one thing to focus your attention on.

What is one little thing you can do right now that will move you in the right direction toward your goal? Perhaps it is something you'll *stop* doing.

It is easy to come up with one simple thing that will add value to your life and start you on your way. Just one little thing.

Often, we think that because our goals are big, we have to take big steps. But that, too, is a trick of the mind. It is the little things you do, day in and day out, that add up to big things over time.

Consider becoming a millionaire. That's a great goal! We all want to be millionaires. But you have no idea how to get there. You don't know how to make a million dollars; you make a modest living. You cannot conceive of having a million dollars given your salary and your spending habits.

So you play the lottery, hoping and praying that you'll win and that will be the answer to your prayers. Or you try any and every get-rich-quick scheme that you can find. There are so many of those available, and new ones come out all the time!

These methods make you think that it's possible to achieve great success without doing the work, without taking the action needed to achieve results. Because you dream of it and want it so badly, you feel entitled to have the outcome without doing the work, so you try to find a shortcut to the outcome you seek. This leads to discouragement and the accompanying emotions, including anger and resentment. You are not achieving the success you want, and you are not happy.

Some people do make money this way—conning and scamming others into playing their game and buying into their scheme. *They* make money, but you struggle. While they may become rich, they have to live with the hurt they cause others. Because they are not living with integrity and honesty, there will be a debt for them to pay in some way. There is a lesson to be learned that will present itself in due time. There are no shortcuts to success.

A million dollars is one million one-dollar bills. Do you have access to one-dollar bills? Of course you do! If you were to start accumulating them, especially in some sort of investment where they gain interest and you earn money on your money, then eventually, you would have a million dollars. It may take many years making small deposits, but so long as you keep adding to the investment, you will eventually achieve your goal.

Small Steps Produce Big Results

During a coaching session, a client admitted that her doctor wants her to consider bariatric surgery or lose one hundred pounds. She was pretty stressed about this and thoughts about it were intruding on her work.

What would you do if your doctor told you to lose one hundred pounds or change your lifestyle in some way to avoid negative health consequences? Perhaps you've never tried to lose weight before; you've always just eaten whatever you wanted and didn't really pay attention until a precipitating event awakened you to your reality, as happened to my client. (You got "whacked" on the side of the head!) Your health has started to suffer, and your doctor advised that if you don't change now, it will only get worse for you. Your doctor cares about you.

What do you do?

If you approach this by looking at the end result, you see the problem as a huge mountain you must climb. In this case, my client was looking at losing one hundred pounds and was becoming totally overwhelmed. It was too big of a mountain to climb.

Whatever your goal, break it down into smaller goals and then create an action plan with steps to achieve that first goal. Focus on small steps you can take today or this week. Whether your goal involves completing a work project, conducting a job search, writing a novel, or regaining your health, break the larger goal into smaller goals, focusing on what you can do, what you have time to do, what you have the resources to do now. This will make it easier for you to take action and get started on your journey.

Big tasks require lots of small steps. Small steps produce big results.

For my client, regaining her health would likely require the assistance of a professional and was outside the scope of our work together. However, as a leader, we were able to explore how she tackles big projects at work and compare that process to how she might approach this in a similar way. We also reviewed these eight strategies so she could outline the steps needed for her to achieve success.

The goal here is twofold: first, chunk your big goals down into smaller goals so you can take small steps, and second, focus on what you can do, what you have access to right now, and not on what you cannot do.

Small steps produce big results.

My client did not have a plan yet, but there were many things she could do right now to get started. What was she willing to commit to? She could certainly start envisioning her future, healthy, thinner self. What did that look like and feel like? How would she be different in this new vision? What qualities might she need to adopt? What resources will she need to get started?

Climbing the staircase to success requires that we take one step at a time. Start wherever you are.

Choose an action: What one thing would you be willing to do today, this week, this month to get you started on your goal? Instead of focusing on the end result and some future desired outcome, focus on the here and now and choose one thing you could do that would be a step in the direction toward achieving your goal.

Change happens in stages. Little things help to prepare, motivate, and inspire you since they are so easy to do. You do one little thing, and it feels good, so you do something else. Along the way, you change—you think different, act different, and eventually, you become different.

Small steps produce big results.

Don't focus on the big task ahead of you, just the next small step you can take. Don't focus on what you can't do, focus on what you can do right now in the direction you want to go. When you look for little ways to make changes and break it down into small steps, you can easily move forward. Reflect on your actions. Celebrate your success. Acknowledge how easy it was. Then, take another step.

Take Another Step

It's not *one* thing you do that leads to success; it is *many* things. It is the little things you do day in and day out in a myriad of ways that eventually lead you to victory. Persistence is a key ingredient. You have to "keep on keeping on"; keep taking small steps over and over again until you have "eaten the entire elephant" (or had your dissertation signed by the dean!).

Always take another step. There will be forces at work to hold you back and roadblocks to interfere with your progress, most of which are in your own head! While there may be some roadblocks along the way, few outside forces conspire to keep you from your goal. Where there is commitment, you will find a way.

In fact, when you are committed, it is as if forces conspire to support you and your efforts. Resources and opportunities find their way to you, and suddenly, you have everything you need to take that next step.

The phenomenon of having things appear just as you need them to or having things fall easily and neatly into place is known as synchronicity. There is no reason to believe that synchronicity will not happen if you are doing what you need to do to respect yourself and honor your talent and abilities.

Sometimes, the path you have chosen is not working to help you achieve your goal. You seem to keep hitting a wall. Persist by seeking a new path—don't be attached to continuing one path to achieve your goal if it's not working. Accept your reality. Be open to possibilities and trust that a new door will open for you. But if you keep walking into the wall thinking that is how you are supposed to "persist," it is as if you are committed to walking into walls.

Stop walking into walls! Stop struggling!

Change course. Try something new. Revisit your plan of action. Perhaps you need more information or education about how to proceed. Perhaps you need a new resource, teacher, or coach to help you on your way. Or perhaps you need a new plan of action. Don't keep doing what you've always done. Let go of the way you've always done it. Remain committed to your goal and open yourself up to the possibility that there is another way to get there, and you are not yet familiar with it. Take some time off. Relax. Eventually the answers will come so you can take that next step.

Avoidance Behaviors

There are things you do to avoid taking action. Do you know what they are? Do you escape into TV or work? Do you daydream? Perhaps you overschedule and overcommit to ensure you have absolutely no time. *Ten minutes to work out, are you kidding me?*

Your stories are ways to avoid taking action. *I can't do that because I have a bad back. Bad knees. The doctor told me not to.* These are just excuses for why you don't. Our stories and excuses are everywhere. They offer us reasons to avoid taking action, and they become limiting beliefs, which are habits of thought that limit our success. They are the little ways in which we lie to ourselves. We play these games under the pretext of keeping us safe when, in fact, they keep us from taking care of ourselves. This is your ego at work.

Why do you avoid taking action on your behalf? You avoid taking actions that you associate with feelings of discomfort. If the action is coupled with feelings of distress or angst, then you won't do it. If you feel fearful and uncomfortable, if you feel something is hard, a chore, and you hate it, you won't do it. You avoid when you do not perceive the results as offering great enough value or reward to motivate you to perform the tasks required to get those results. Hence, you are not yet committed, your vision is not compelling enough to motivate you, or you do not believe in the possibility for success.

Commitment means you will go to any lengths, do whatever it takes to achieve the desired results. If you avoid taking action, then you are resistant. You are struggling with your inner demons, and they are winning.

Identify your avoidance behaviors and the thoughts behind those behaviors. Pay attention to your resistance and the ways in which you attempt to avoid and escape from doing the things you need to do to move forward with your change. Become aware so you can accept responsibility for your behavior and your choices. If you avoid taking action, do it consciously and intentionally. Don't just make excuses for not doing something.

The only reason to avoid doing something, besides not being ready, is because of fear. Name your fear. Get it out into the open and do whatever it is you need to do to move you forward. Get the right support and take a little, baby step.

Once you take that first step beyond your fear, congratulate yourself, and then take another step. Eventually, you will rise above that fear. You will take charge. You will develop your courage muscles. You can do it! And as you celebrate your accomplishments (which we will cover in chapter 12, strategy 6) you will become motivated to keep moving toward your goal.

Focus on What Is Right in Front of You

You become overwhelmed and frightened because you are focused on the destination. You want to finish that degree. You want to create that amazing relationship. You want to be a better leader. You want that promotion. You want those million dollars!

With so much of your attention and energy going to the end result, you become discouraged because you don't yet have it and it seems so far away. You become attached to the outcome you desire so much so that you neglect this moment and what is right in front of you.

The only way to get there is to start here. If you want to run a marathon, you need to get some running shoes. Then you need to start running. But if you have never run before, you may only be able to run a short distance before your body says, "What do you think you're doing? Cut it out!" And you can't run any longer.

If you never go out running again, then you have given up on your goal. But if tomorrow you try again, perhaps you will be able to run a little farther and a little faster. After several weeks, you are running two miles and then three. Eventually, you will be able to run that marathon.

You may not have those million dollars today, but you can meet with a financial advisor, create a plan of action, and start saving—one dollar at a time.

Start where you are.

You may want to be a better communicator. Start with your next conversation. Ask more questions. Be curious about how the other person thinks. Keep the focus on them rather than you. Afterward, reflect on how you did. How did it feel to have that conversation? How did the other person feel while speaking with you? Did they feel heard? If you are not sure, then when wrapping up start asking people what value they received from the conversation and if there is anything else they need. Learn ways to improve with each conversation.

Too much energy is wasted focusing on the outcome rather than the process. You focus on the fantasy rather than the reality of the here and now. By focusing on doing what you need to do and enjoying the process, you begin to find happiness on the journey as opposed to thinking that happiness only occurs when you arrive at your destination. The journey to success is your life. If you are not enjoying the journey, but only wishing for and working for the end result, then you miss the joy and the fun that exists in this day, this moment, this experience.

Action happens in this moment. Today is all you have. Do with it what you can. Focus your attention on the job at hand and the small steps you can take now, and let tomorrow be there for you when you get to it. When you focus on the action steps you can take today and move beyond your fear to take those steps, you focus on what you can control, and you experience less stress. Then, you can let go and trust that the outcome and the future will take care of itself.

A Return to Trust

Old habits and neurological connections don't die; they weaken. Just like muscles that have atrophied or weakened from lack of use, they will strengthen should you start to work them out again regularly.

When you change, at first you are excited and energized. You go after what you want with gusto. You are committed to the new life you envision. You take action and start to see the results.

If you are not careful, however, if you do not continue to pay attention, you can become discouraged, falter, and slip back into old ways (habits). Change requires consistency over time. You have to walk this new path until it becomes second nature, until it becomes a habit, which can take many months.

Do not lose sight of your vision. Do not forget your commitment. You must consistently and constantly ask yourself what you value and make choices that coincide with the future you are trying to create. Like sailing a boat at sea, keep one eye on the horizon (your vision) and the other on navigating your boat (the actions you can take today). You also want to look back to see how far you have traveled and celebrate how far you have come. We will discuss this further in chapter 12, strategy 6.

It is not hard to stay on task; it is just easy to fall back into old habits. Staying focused requires awareness and vigilance. You may get tired. If you stay focused long enough and if you reinforce the accomplishments and progress you are making by celebrating your successes and relishing the changes you've made to date, you will continue along the path. You will remember that going back is not an option—failure is not an option. You are committed to this new life. And again, you recommit to the vision you are inspired to create.

Remember where you came from and why you embarked upon this change to begin with. What motivated you? What was the pain you were experiencing and the pleasure you were seeking?

Remember, too, all the work required to achieve the results you enjoy today.

In addiction recovery, they call this process "keeping it green." You remember what it was like "when" . . .

- when you were using drugs,
- when you were overweight,
- when you were in debt,
- when you were alone/single,
- when you were stressed out and overworked,
- when you were so reactionary and lacked control of your emotions,
- when you were so overwhelmed because you would not delegate.

The key here to remember is that *now* you have a choice. You are aware and in control. You can choose to return to your old ways—if that is what you want—or you can continue to create wonderful, new things for you to enjoy and experience. You are making a conscious choice.

This is very powerful.

You will continue a particular behavior over and over again, not realizing consciously how it is hurting you or damaging you, your relationships, or your ability to experience love and joy. This is known as your blind spot. As it has been said, "The definition of insanity is doing the same thing over and over and expecting different results." Once you are aware, however, once you wake up from your "unconsciousness," you have the ability to choose how you want to proceed in your life.

Learning to trust yourself takes time. How much time depends upon you and your track record for making and keeping commitments, how well you know yourself, and how committed you are to creating your new life.

However, just like in recovery programs, there may need to be a little reminder every so often to "keep it green" for you. Don't forget where you came from, because it is ever so easy to return if you have not yet learned the lessons that the struggle to change was meant to create.

The Lessons We Must Learn

We are given certain lessons in life to learn from and to help us to develop and grow. This is what having a life experience is about. We navigate through life by learning, growing, teaching, loving, and experiencing different things. Along the way, we are presented with lessons. And if we learn what the lesson is teaching us, we grow and are offered new lessons. If we do not learn and grow, then the lesson repeats until we finally get it.

Life is hard because we resist the lessons. We behave like a two-year-old, stomping and kicking our feet because we don't like what is presenting itself, and we resist learning what the lesson is teaching us.

What we resist persists.

The practice of accepting and letting go of the attachments to your own ideas about how life should be helps to lessen the burden and struggle of change. You will have pain. If you love, the pain of the loss you experience will be proportionate to the amount that you love. But the loss of one thing or person begets the space for something new to enter.

We are not always open to the idea that there could be something else waiting for us. We cannot envision it, so we believe it must not exist. This is small thinking. We are greater than our own thoughts.

We are quite limited in our own mind. Those fifty thousand thoughts we have every day are only a smidgen of the knowing that is possible.

Suspend Your Judgment

Do not compare or judge others on their path to success. You may witness people lose weight only to gain it again. You hear stories of bankruptcy, and the next time you see the person, you witness them whipping out their credit card to make a large purchase.

Now, you understand why it is so easy to slip back into old patterns of behavior, and you will start to see its evidence everywhere. People have to learn the lessons they are meant to learn from the hardships that have been presented to them. If they do not learn the lesson, the lesson repeats itself over and over again until the person understands what the lesson is trying to teach them and learns from it.

Only then will they move on to the next lesson.

"But for the grace of God, there go I." In other words, that could be you. We are all mirrors for each other. There is no reason to judge; it feels bad when others do it to us. Instead, we can give others grace as they struggle to navigate their life.

We all have to learn about love and money and material things. We all have to learn how to master our emotions and care for ourselves and keep a job, put food on the table, take care of our families, and save for retirement. We have to deal with death, taxes, and health. We each have bodies that require our attention. We all have to figure out this life thing. This is part of being human.

Suspend your judgment of others. Give them the grace you would like given to you as you travel your difficulties. Accept that they, too, have their own fears, walls, attachments, and inner demons that they battle with every day. Sometimes, they lose the fight. Be grateful for your own demons; you wouldn't want to trade for anyone else's!

Slow and Steady Wins the Race

"You must never confuse faith that you will prevail in the end—which you can never afford to lose—with the discipline to confront the most brutal facts of your current reality, whatever they might be."

—*Admiral James Stockdale*

I cannot tell you how many times over the years I have questioned my chosen path. I cannot tell you how many times I wondered if success was possible, if I was doing the right things, following the right path. Each time, I was being tested for my commitment to whatever it was I was seeking, whether it was my health, leading others effectively, coaching masterfully, getting out of debt, finding a soulmate, or succeeding in business. *Am I making a difference? Is this the right path? Should I try something new? What do my staff or my clients want of me? Is this what I want to be doing? Is there another way?*

We question our commitment, then recommit and take another step.

Persistence and resilience have been the greatest strategies for my success. When I fall, I stand up and take yet another step. *Failure is not falling; it's lying there.* If you don't succeed at first, keep trying.

Many a millionaire went bankrupt before they figured out how to become rich. They had to first learn how to fall down before they could learn to sustain the result.

You can focus on your obstacles or your fear or how far you have yet to travel; you can stay attached to your thoughts and fantasies about how life should be; or you can focus on taking actions that will add value to your life. You can listen to others complain about how hard it is, or you can embrace the belief that it can be easy and take another step toward victory.

It may seem like the steps you are taking are not getting you anywhere; remember that eating an elephant or taking a journey of a thousand miles will take longer than a day, perhaps longer than you expect. Trust that so long as you are taking the right steps, you are moving in the right direction.

Small steps produce big results.

We may want quick results, but life operates at its own pace. You don't have to like it. I often don't! I want things to happen sooner, but the uncomfortable feeling I experience when it takes longer than I think it should informs me that this is a lesson I still must learn. I also know that happiness is an inside job. It is to be experienced in the here and now, not at some destination or point in the future. If I cannot enjoy what I am experiencing *now*, how will I enjoy what is to come? I will not know how to be happy if I cannot be content in this moment.

Every obstacle, every struggle you face is an opportunity to learn and to grow and to stretch yourself. And this you must do in order to achieve the success you desire. A slow and steady pace helps you win the race. It does you no good to run so fast you cannot enjoy your journey, or, when you do arrive at your destination—if you get there—you are so burned out and unhealthy you are unable to enjoy the fruits of your labor.

It is easy to take one small step. Take another step toward victory and enjoy the process as you journey to your new life. Joy is found in the journey; the achievement itself is fleeting. We will discuss this further with strategy 7. But first, let's explore the importance of celebrating our success along the way with strategy 6.

CHAPTER 12

STRATEGY 6: CELEBRATE YOUR SUCCESS ALONG THE WAY

---

*"The more you praise and celebrate your life,
the more there is in life to celebrate."*

—Oprah Winfrey

Pat Yourself on the Back

During a recent conversation, a friend who is participating in a weight loss program complained that she had reached a plateau. She had not budged for a few days.

She seemed disappointed; however, she had lost fifteen pounds. I reminded her of that and congratulated her on her amazing success. She thanked me. All she could see was what she hadn't accomplished; she was not looking at what she had already achieved. This is a benefit of having a supportive community.

All too often we focus on the road ahead of us and forget to acknowledge everything we do day in and day out to have gotten this far. It is so easy to see only what we have not yet done and become disappointed. We get lost in negative thoughts that beat us up and put us down. We forget how important it is to achieve this goal. We forget all of the work we have put into it to date. We get depressed and give up.

Discouragement sets in when you see only how far you have yet to go. To prevent discouragement and to stay focused, motivated, and engaged in making your vision a reality, celebrate and congratulate yourself at every opportunity.

Every time you laugh instead of cry or scream, acknowledge yourself. Every time you save that dollar instead of spending it, every time you remain curious and ask questions in conversation instead of telling the person what to do, give yourself a pat on the back. Every time you make good food choices, congratulate yourself and reinforce your commitment to your health. Let the scale take care of itself. If you do all the right things, you will benefit, you will make progress, and you will succeed.

Every time you make a positive choice in the right direction, make a mental acknowledgment. Share it with your community or coach. Pat yourself on the back. We don't do this enough. We don't acknowledge ourselves, our progress, or our successes.

It is crucial to acknowledge your accomplishments, even the smallest changes, so you see the progress you are making. It helps motivate you to keep going, to keep taking that next step. It feels good to witness yourself make good choices. This adds to your confidence, reinforces your commitment, and encourages you to do more.

Each small step on your journey to change is significant. It allows you to take the next one and moves you along your path. It demonstrates that you are making different choices and building new habits. Therefore, each step is important.

When you turn around to look behind you at how far you have traveled, you can see your progress. You can rejoice that you are no longer where you were. You may not be where you want to be yet, but you are not where you were anymore.

Often, we put too much pressure on the result rather than the process. By celebrating and acknowledging the steps you take, it keeps you focused on the journey and the process rather than the outcome or destination.

Acknowledgment doesn't necessarily mean you have to *do* anything; you simply take a moment to soak in the fact that you are working hard. You are doing it! You are taking this journey.

There can be a reward, but there doesn't have to be.

It is too easy for us to focus on the negative. You know exactly when you don't do what you are supposed to. You beat yourself up for hours, even days, when you make a mistake. The guilt forces you into depression and leads you to be self-deprecating.

This can often have a negative effect on your continuing your goal. *Well, I ate poorly today, so I might as well give up.* Or *I became very frantic and overwhelmed today at work. I cannot be a leader. Who am I fooling?*

Learning to accept when you make mistakes and regress into old habits is part of the process and is to be expected! If you expect yourself to never mess up, then you are practicing perfectionism. "Perfect" is an illusion. What is perfection anyway? Strive to do your best—to be perfectly imperfect. Look for progress, not perfection.

Expect to mess up. Congratulate yourself on noticing that you behaved in a manner that is no longer aligned with your new life— your new *you*. Acknowledge it, laugh about it, apologize if you need to, and move on. Get back on track.

Spend more time celebrating success every day rather than finding fault. If you focus on things you do wrong, you will amplify them, and your thoughts will get the better of you. If you focus on things you do right and what you do well, you will improve them. You will choose to do more because you will want to move toward pleasure. The more you take pleasure in success, the more excited you become and the more willing you are to work diligently toward achieving your goal.

Along your quest for success, you are learning how to be great. You are growing, developing, and evolving. As you acknowledge yourself and your wins, your confidence increases, you become more comfortable with the new you that you are creating, and you begin to bring down your wall.

A Member of Club Human

> *"To make no mistakes is not in the power of man;*
> *but from their errors and mistakes the wise and*
> *good learn wisdom for the future."*

—Plutarch

Things happen. You'll make mistakes. That's life. You will slip back into old patterns of behavior. You will raise your voice, eat that piece of chocolate cake, and give in to that request for overtime even though you wanted to spend time with your family.

You will run into brick walls sometimes. When you realize you've hit a wall, stop, and change direction. Don't continue to walk into the wall. It's frustrating and stressful.

Mistakes bring your attention to something. If you feel guilty, then perhaps you are not being honest with yourself; there is a layer of denial to peel away. Perhaps you are not respecting yourself and your commitment in some way. Revisit your commitment, your priorities, your values, and your vision. What are you missing?

Perhaps you didn't realize that you didn't know something. Great! You now have the opportunity to learn from this so you can avoid repeating it in the future. You don't know what you don't know until somehow it gets pointed out to you.

Often, you can learn about a mistake from your emotional responses. Notice the emotion and name it. What is the message?

- Are you feeling fear over taking a particular action? Is it real fear telling you to wait, or is it False Evidence Appearing Real?

- Do you feel guilty working overtime instead of spending time with your family? Are you practicing avoidance or escape behavior?

- Are you nervous or anxious about an interaction with another person? Is there a conversation you need to have to address a boundary, clear the air, or to make amends?

- What is the story that is running through your head? Is it grounded in reality or a fantasy you are making up? Is it true? What assumptions are you making in this situation?

Apologizing can be very therapeutic and can help mend relationships and build trust. It shows tremendous courage and inner strength to admit a mistake, and it demonstrates leadership to accept responsibility for your actions.

You don't always need to apologize for mistakes or errors. Oftentimes, the only person you hurt is yourself. So what if you had a piece of chocolate? So what if your conversation turned into you telling that person what to do instead of asking for their thoughts and ideas? If you fall, no big deal. Just get up and start over. Notice and observe your thoughts, feelings, and behaviors. Learn from them. Recommit to the changes you want to make. And do your best to avoid making the same mistake again.

Next time you are offered a similar opportunity, consider your options; try each option on to see how it feels. Which choice feels better for you? Which choice is in alignment with your vision and commitment? Which adds the greatest value to you? What are the potential consequences of your choice, and who will be impacted? Is this acceptable to you? If you know that making a particular choice will make you feel bad or bring on feelings of guilt and shame, and you fear the repercussions, then don't do it!

Taking a moment to consider the emotional reaction you might anticipate to each of your options helps you to make better decisions.

If you are moving toward pleasure and away from pain, then don't choose things that will bring on feelings of fear and guilt and pain! Do only those things for which the consequences are what you seek and that feel right for you.

Hearing the Good Stuff

Whereas some people have no trouble giving compliments, others are quite stingy with praise. We definitely could benefit from acknowledging each other more often.

Most people, however, have a hard time receiving compliments and hearing "the good stuff." Often, when I ask clients to share their accomplishments and tell me their strengths, they hesitate. It feels uncomfortable, embarrassing. They either don't know, or they have difficulty talking about it.

Somewhere along the way, you may have been taught that it was egotistical or wrong to acknowledge the wonderful things about you. It is boasting or rude. Perhaps you are just so accustomed to hearing the bad stuff or so used to focusing on other people that you have never really taken the time to notice all that you do—all that you are—and celebrate it.

It is not egotistical to acknowledge what you do well. Boasting occurs when you compare yourself to others in order to lift up your self-esteem and put others down, or when you feel the need to tell everyone how wonderful you are. To simply acknowledge your strengths and acknowledgments is actually quite important for your development and growth and for your success and enjoyment.

Observe yourself as you truly are. See the good along with the bad. If all you ever see is the bad and the mistakes, how will you know you are on the right track? When do you get to be satisfied? When does "good" ever happen if you won't acknowledge it? Do you ever get to be good? When does success come if you cannot recognize it and take pleasure in it?

Consider the choices you make and the actions you take, and when they add value, when they make you feel good, when you feel as though you are respecting and honoring yourself, then pat yourself on the back. It's okay.

Change takes time, longer than you want it to, so every day you take action, you move closer to your goal and closer to becoming the person you dream of becoming. Congratulations. Small steps produce big results. Squash discouragement by acknowledging the small steps you take every day to create change. Then you can focus on taking the next step.

Success Comes in Stages

"Success is not a doorway, it's a staircase."

—*Dottie Walters*

You are standing on a step on your staircase to success. You see your destination in the future. But you are not there; you're here. You want to be farther up the stairs, but for some reason, you are stuck on this step. And you don't like it.

Welcome to the plateau. It won't last; nothing does. How you handle the plateau, however, speaks volumes about your character: Do you rest and recover from your climb? Do you focus on preparing yourself for the next climb? Do you get frustrated and have a temper tantrum? Do you allow your negative thoughts to get the better of you? *I told you so. You'll never get there!* Do you get depressed? Do you turn back?

We achieve success in stages, much like walking up a flight of stairs. We take a step and then we pause. Then we take another step. The same is true here with our strategy for change. We take a step in the right direction; we notice and acknowledge our good choices. Then we take another step.

We get used to it. It becomes comfortable. We create habits. But we are not yet finished with our climb; we have just achieved another step. We must keep going and take another step.

Over time we can look back to see how far up the stairs we have gone. We can also see how far we have yet to go. At some point, however, you realize that you are no longer where you were—you are no longer in debt; you are debt free. You are no longer losing weight; you are maintaining a healthy weight. You are no longer sick; you are now healthy. You are no longer looking for love; you have found it—or it has found you. You have finally achieved that promotion or changed jobs (or careers).

You have reached a new level of achievement. Embrace this moment. It is a pivotal moment in your life. Drink in the moment because this too shall pass. Success is fleeting. Enjoy it and then prepare yourself; it will be time to change again soon.

There is a moment when you realize that you are no longer a child; you are an adult. There is another moment when you acknowledge that you are no longer a novice but rather a professional, perhaps even an expert in your field. When you become a leader, you realize you are no longer an individual contributor but rather now a manager of individual contributors.

In that instant, acknowledge your accomplishment. Recognize how much effort it took to achieve this step. Celebrate you! You are amazing! You have come so far on your journey of a thousand miles!

People often struggle with this step. People have difficulty acknowledging the work, time, dedication, and fortitude—the talent and skill—required for them to get to this place. You did it! This is what you have worked for. Take the time to savor the moment. Soon enough, you'll start to wonder what's next. There is another step to take, other accomplishments to reach, other mountains to climb. This is just a pit stop on your journey.

How long will you be on the plateau? Who knows? Don't get stuck here but give yourself permission to enjoy the experience and stay for a while. Recognize how you've grown and acknowledge the person you are becoming.

For now, savor the moment, acknowledge the changes you've made, and take time to rest and reflect, to celebrate and marvel at your greatness.

Practice Gratitude

"Adversity introduces a person to themselves."

—Albert Einstein

As events occur, you can look for the lesson and learn from it. Much research has been done on the practice of gratitude. Gratitude has been shown to increase well-being, enhance positive emotions, make us more optimistic, and potentially improve physical health.

The following story was a very challenging time for me as I escaped death. I cannot quite explain why I felt the way I felt at the time, but I will do my best.

One month after the birth of my son, Josh, I became very ill. I developed ulcerative colitis, a condition where the large intestine ulcerates and bleeds. This is a very painful, debilitating illness. For sixteen months, I did not know health. There were no good days and bad days; only very sick days and tolerable days. By the end, I would spend twenty-six days in the hospital and require two major surgeries to survive.

At the time, I was married to my first husband, John. The ordeal proved to be too much for our relationship, and we divorced soon after my second surgery. Remember, we had a newborn at home, and I relied on John to care for our son while I focused on staying alive. Sickness takes a toll on relationships.

Life is like this. We all have our stories.

The strange part of the story is that throughout this time, I felt an enormous amount of gratitude. I cannot explain it. I was grateful that it was me who was sick and not my son; so much can happen to either mother or child during and after pregnancy. Josh was perfectly healthy, and for that I was very grateful.

I was grateful that I was not going to die. I knew I had a way to live. I was grateful for the experience, I guess. If there was something I did—in this life or another—to deserve this experience and pain, then I was grateful for the opportunity to pay my debt.

I was grateful for the amazing team of surgeons who saved my life and the nurses and other members of the healthcare team who cared for me. And even though I could see that my marriage would end when I was stable, I was very grateful that John was able to care for our son while I suffered through this ordeal. I honestly don't know what I would have done without him at the time.

Through this horrible time of my life, I felt "carried." I was prepared to handle it. There were synchronistic events that occurred, and I was navigated to the right resources at the right time in order to have the experience I was meant to have. I learned so much during my ordeal, which I am sure has contributed greatly to the person I am today.

When you experience this kind of life-threatening illness or adversity, you learn how fragile life is and not to take anything for granted. Each day is a gift. You never know how much time you have, which is why it is so important to live each day to the fullest so that when you do reach the end, you feel good about the time you did have.

We waste so much time wishing things were different and fighting our reality rather than doing what we can do and enjoying what we have.

Be grateful for everything in your life. Acknowledge all the wonderful things you do and celebrate all your achievements. If something does not bring you joy, then change it or change your attitude toward it. Don't just put up with it. What might you need to learn? Life is too short to be unhappy for long.

We each have a purpose. You are here in this lifetime to give the best of yourself to a world that desperately needs you. Stop hiding behind your fears or your wall. Stop giving in to discouragement. Show yourself and others love, respect, acceptance, and understanding. Let go of things that don't serve you. Open yourself up to possibilities that life can be wonderful and fun, filled with laughter and love—because it CAN! Life is what you make of it.

The Declaration of Independence ensures us of the three inalienable rights to life, liberty, and the pursuit of happiness. Although we have the right to *pursue* happiness, as Benjamin Franklin stated, "You have to go catch it for yourself."

No one else can make you happy. Happiness is an inside job. You have to discover it for yourself. When you celebrate your successes, acknowledge the goodness in you and in your achievements, then you begin to experience how amazing and wonderful you are. In this world of craziness, with so many choices and so much misery and unhappiness, there is still hope for change. There is still a desire and hunger for peace and for a better world. And it all starts with you.

CHAPTER 13

STRATEGY 7:
LAUGH AND ENJOY
THE JOURNEY

"Above all else: go out with a sense of humor. It is needed armor. Joy in one's heart and some laughter on one's lips is a sign that the person down deep has a pretty good grasp of life."

—Hugh Sidey

Lighten Up

We take ourselves so seriously, don't we? You have been learning about the mind and the tricks it plays to throw you off course. This is another way that fear holds us back; it makes us fear the consequences of our actions, so we hold back and hide behind our walls. By using the need to be right, attachment to our ideas, incessant self-questioning and doubt, harsh personal judgment, avoidance behaviors, and the expectation for things to be a certain way, fear grips us with emotions that cause us to freeze. We resist. This becomes all powerful and consuming and holds us back from being ourselves, enjoying life, experiencing great relationships, accepting new ways of doing things, and allowing life to unfold as it will.

Things we think are important often are not. Things we fight for (and will fight to the death for) are often just ideas in our minds. We hurt people we care about in order to get our point across. At the end of our life, however, the only things we remember are the hurt we caused, the love we shared, and the love we lost.

So we laugh. We laugh to lighten the mood. We laugh to loosen the grip of our attachments. We laugh because it reminds us of how silly we can be. We laugh because it puts things in perspective. It forces us to question our values in the moment: What is really important here? Usually, it's not what we are being so darn stubborn about!

We laugh because it is healthy, and it adds value to our bodies. It releases chemicals that make us feel good. We laugh to make others realize that they are also being too serious, and they need to lighten up as well!

Laughter helps us face anything. It is great medicine. With a little humor, we can swallow just about any pill life shoves at us. Without the ability to laugh and to enjoy our days, life becomes quite stale, and we become stoic.

Life is meant to be savored; if you cannot laugh, how can you take delight in all the beauty and wonder around you?

Laughter Is Great Medicine

Laughter lifts your spirits; in so doing, it decreases your stress. People who laugh a lot tend to feel good about themselves and about life. They report good health, a general sense of well-being, and a brighter outlook on life.

Studies correlate laughter and humor with good health. Laughter is a physical activity that causes endorphins to be released and more oxygen to enter your bloodstream as the act of laughing expands your lungs. You also burn calories when you laugh. Laughter therapy is used for cancer patients and people suffering from other illnesses. Clowns are often invited to children's hospitals to help children stay focused on living as opposed to being sick. Laughter takes your mind off of your pain so you can enjoy the moment. In the end, moments are all we have in which we can experience joy and happiness.

It's good to be silly. It feels good to let loose a little. A good sense of humor keeps relationships strong and deepens the connections and bonds between people.

At the start of our relationship, there were times when my dear husband, Lou, would get onto his little pedestal with his need to be right. I would feel myself pulling back and recognized this wall separating us. In these moments, he was not open to sharing; he was focused on telling. I became familiar with this feeling and would smile and make a little joke about his need to be right: "Oh, so is this you needing to be right?" He would laugh! Then we could engage in a more productive conversation, one in which I could participate.

Laughter helped to bridge the wall that separated us. Lou learned to recognize when my need to be right emerged, and he would do something similar for me. Together, we learned to respect each other's needs, which helped cradle our delicate self-esteem, while at the same time learning ways to communicate more effectively and connect more deeply. Over time, this occurred less and less frequently; in fact, I cannot remember the last time this wall emerged.

In her book *Growing Up Laughing: My Story and the Story of Funny*, Marlo Thomas talks about what it was like for her to grow up with laughter as the core of her home environment. Some people have angst; her family had laughter. And with laughter, she and her siblings grew up learning the importance of having a sense of humor and the impact it has on experiencing and enjoying life. When you laugh, you are having fun. And, as Alan Alda of the show *M*A*S*H* said, "When people are laughing, they are generally not killing each other."

Are You Having Fun Yet?

"How we spend our days is, of course, how we spend our lives."

—*Annie Dillard*

Without laughter, we become lost in our thoughts. Laughter helps us break free from our mental barrage.

With laughter, you can learn to have fun doing just about anything. After all, you make tough choices about how you spend your time. You trade your time for something of value. Why would you then not enjoy yourself?

If you are not doing things that you enjoy, is it because you really don't enjoy doing those things, or is it because you really don't know how to enjoy yourself doing anything?

Some of us need to learn how to have fun. In your quest to find your path in life, you may not have learned to let loose and have a good time on your journey. You may not know what "having a good time" means! What a great place to be! It's great because once you realize this, you can decide to do something different and start on the path of adding fun to your life.

Adding fun and learning to laugh are skills you can develop. Start small by watching funny movies, sitcoms, or the comedy channel. Read jokes or comic strips. Smile more often throughout your day; give your facial muscles a workout. There are many little things to laugh at instead of getting angry, like laughing when your baby spits up on you or when your husband wants the remote back. Tickle your son or daughter before they go to bed. Children love to laugh! They know how to be silly. In fact, spending time with children is very therapeutic. They'll teach you how to have fun!

Kids are so wonderful; they really do enjoy themselves. Watch them play and use their imagination. Marvel at how their young minds work.

Somewhere along the way, they learn to be more serious; that is, adults teach them they need to be serious about their schoolwork, get into college or trade school, and find a job. We want them to be responsible and make good choices. We teach them these things, and we squash the fun and the imagination right out of them.

These children then grow up to be us! They become adults who are chasing after the money, the job, the house, the kids, the partner/spouse; running to keep up with the Joneses; trying to impress people to build their self-worth; questioning if they are doing okay; wondering if this is all life is about; and wishing it didn't have to be so hard.

Fear keeps you anxious and scared and hidden behind your wall. You question and doubt yourself. You are insecure about what to do, how to do it, and what other people will think. Laughter helps you to bring down that wall. What happened to you in the past does not need to be repeated in the present. Being an adult means embracing your freedom to make decisions. Creating the changes you wish to make means choosing to do things that are fun for you and learning to have fun doing everything you choose.

If you are having fun doing what you are doing, you will be motivated to continue. Laughter motivates. If you are not having fun, if you dread what you are doing, you are dreading your life. Whenever someone mentions not liking Mondays, I cringe! What is wrong with Mondays? If you hate Mondays, then you hate nearly 15 percent of your life. What else do you hate?

You can learn to structure your life so that every day, you are doing things you love with people you enjoy and who bring out your best. First envision what you want, believe in the possibility for success, and begin to eliminate things that you don't like while choosing to do things you enjoy. Learn more in my first book, *The Journey Called YOU: A Roadmap to Self-Discovery and Acceptance,* where you can learn to use the Time Enjoyment Model©, a four-quadrant model for learning to balance your time with what you are skilled at and what you enjoy. Imagine looking forward to Mondays as much as any other day of the week!

Beware the Laughter Wall

"Gaiety is not proof that the heart is at ease, for often in the midst of laughter the heart is sad."

—Stephanie Genlis

There are times when you may use laughter as an avoidance behavior. Behind the laugh, behind the humor, you hide your pain. This is your wall. It is quite evident; a careful observer will see the pain in your eyes.

While the jokes and the laughter help you deny your pain effectively, keeping you from facing what ails you, it still hurts. No amount of laughter can rid you of pain. If there is something you must face, face it. What you resist persists. It will keep coming back to haunt you until you acknowledge whatever message the emotion is trying to bring to your attention.

Do not fear this emotion. Do not resist. Deal with it. Find a safe environment in order to face it. Reach out to someone such as a coach, friend, your partner or spouse, or a therapist. Do not let resistance win. It will keep you in pain, and your pain will prevent you from living a full and free life. You will be imprisoned by this pain and your fear of it.

There is nothing that is so bad that you cannot face it. I have heard many stories over the years. And I have some of my own. You blame yourself so harshly that the guilt and shame keep you walled up. This shame then impacts your self-esteem and, over time, thickens the wall between you and others. You fear what people would think "if they only knew." You twist things in your mind in order to make sense of them. Then you craft a story and live with it as if it is truth.

This doesn't make your perspective truth; just your own version of it. Your stories keep you stuck.

When something happens that makes you feel uncomfortable, and you are unsure of your interpretation of the situation, ask someone else to help you talk it through—a trusted friend, colleague, or your therapist or coach. Check in on your stories and your emotions. It may be that you are catastrophizing—blowing things out of proportion. I do that sometimes too. Your feelings, however, bring your attention to something that may have a message for you. Find a way to sort out what that message means for you.

Sometimes, others will validate you. Other times, they may not. They may try to minimize the situation or your emotions by saying that you are overreacting.

Maybe you are, but do not minimize or deny what you feel. Check in and then speak up. Perhaps you did misunderstand the intention; many disagreements and bad feelings begin with misinterpretation. Do not assume that the other person knows what you feel; tell them. Give them a chance to explain themselves and let them know the impact their behavior or words had on you. By hearing one another out and sharing honestly and openly about how you feel and what you need, you keep your relationships healthy and clear of negative feelings.

Your interpretation or the thoughts you have about a situation create the story you live by. Do not be attached to your story. Deal with the emotions to eliminate the negative energy you are carrying so it no longer hurts. Stop carrying your past with you into your present. When you eliminate the emotional energy associated with the event, you can tell the story without feeling anything. This is how you know you have dealt with it, and it no longer has a grip on you.

Beware of your superficial laughter. If you would rather cry than laugh, then have your cry and ask yourself what is really going on here for you: identify both the emotion and its trigger. What happened to cause this emotional response? What is the message it has for you? What do you need to do to respect yourself?

So What?

I was turning left onto a fairly busy street when a woman came around the corner and had to slow down while I completed my turn. I watched her throw her arms up in frustration as if saying to me, "What are you doing?"

How frustrated do you become with other people's behavior? How much do you let it bother you? A client asked me about road rage and if I thought screaming and gesturing in his car was a good emotional outlet or a waste of time. This led to an enlightening exploration of expectations and judgment.

Why bother getting yourself so upset about little things over which you have no control? Why go there in the first place so that your heart rate goes up, your blood pressure spikes, and your stress levels rise? It is not healthy to do this consistently. You put yourself at risk for serious health concerns.

Ask yourself, *So what?* Does it matter in the scheme of things if someone is turning left, and you have to slow down a bit? Can you imagine a time when you behaved in a similar fashion? If you drive a car, then you have to turn left sometimes too. Look how quick you are to judge others as "wrong" or "bad" when they do it. Who cares? Who cares if you have to slow down to let someone in or let them pass? At the end of the day, does it really matter? If you had an accident, that would matter a whole lot. But you're safe. Why get yourself so worked up about what others are doing?

What people remember is how you made them feel, how you treated them. Be nice. Empathize by putting yourself in their shoes. Understand that they too have children waiting to be picked up, they too have a job to get to, and they too want to make the green light. It's not such a big deal, but your mind can take it to the extreme.

As for the lady that day, I smiled and sent her positive thoughts for peace and calm. I hope it helped her to relax and enjoy her travels.

If you can catch yourself before you are swept into the drama in your mind, before the emotion sets in, ask yourself *So what?* to consider the importance and relevance of the emotion. For example, if you fear a certain outcome or situation occurring, ask yourself, *What if what I fear does, in fact, happen? So what? What will that mean to my life? Do I have the resources to handle it? What would I do?*

If you don't have the resources to handle situations and setbacks, then perhaps you are living with too much risk. This is wonderful information! Now you can take responsibility for decreasing your risk, so you feel more comfortable and have less stress and fear.

This kind of questioning respects your fear by asking it to explain itself. Is there something valid to the fear? Perhaps you need to listen to it. Perhaps there is something you need to admit to yourself or to prepare for first.

Preparation minimizes risk; it also decreases fear's potency. Fear will show up. Best to prepare for it and welcome the message it brings when it arrives. It's like an unwelcome guest, but a guest nonetheless.

Fear can often feel like intuition. It pretends that it is so important and that there will be consequences if you do not heed the call. This is where acute self-awareness is essential. The difference between fear and intuition is how it feels and where you feel it in your body. Where do you feel your fear? Is it in your stomach or your heart or somewhere else? Once you know what that feels like, then you can more easily recognize it when it shows up again.

Intuition, on the other hand, shows up differently. It will feel different. How do intuitive hits show up for you? For me, it just "comes up" and there is a sense of "knowing." There is no bodily sensation; whereas with fear, I feel it in my chest. Being able to recognize the difference helps you challenge your fear when it masquerades as intuition.

What you resist persists. Challenging your resistance by asking *So what?* helps you to stay in the moment and make better choices about how to spend your time. We can place unrealistic and demanding expectations on ourselves. Does it really matter if you don't vacuum this week or if the laundry waits another day? Will anyone notice or care? So what?

Often, we set very stringent rules for ourselves that no one else holds us to. These can be very stressful and damaging. And when you do not meet your own standards, you judge yourself harshly.

There is no reason for this. Laughter helps you to lighten up and not judge yourself so harshly. Laughter deflates problems and issues to the appropriate size. Things can seem so big when first encountered, but, with laughter, we gain a better perspective.

In ten years' time, will this matter? If so, how will it matter? If not, then what is important about doing this; is it important at all? What is of greatest value to you at this moment?

Live in the Moment

"Life is what happens when we're busy making other plans."

—*John Lennon*

Your habits keep you stuck repeating the past; attachments force you to bring the past into the present; resistance causes you to skip the present; and discouragement makes you regret what isn't real yet. All these barriers to success have to do with either the past or the future. None of them have to do with the here and now. Yet this moment is where your power is; this moment is where happiness lives; this moment is where you experience love and joy. The value of this moment is priceless.

This moment is the most important moment of your life! It is all you have. Use it wisely. Trade it for something of value because you will not have the opportunity to repeat it.

There is urgency to life. One day, you awaken and find yourself fifty—or sixty—and suddenly you begin to realize that life is fragile, and time is limited.

You don't have to wait for that day. Make today the most important day of your life. Be aware of what is important to you. Be clear about your commitments and the vision you have for your future and use this knowledge to help you make good decisions during the course of your day.

Anticipatory fear and anxiety focus on what *could* happen, not what *is* happening. They are about an imaginary future and anticipated results. The present is about this moment, and this moment is what you have control over. When you feel fear or trepidation, pull yourself back into the here and now. The present moment is where you can take action. This is where you have your showdown with fear.

Focus on your vision for success: let that be your beacon as opposed to your fear. Notice your fear, but then focus on being in the now. What do you need to do, say, or ask for? Look around and you will see that fear is trying to remove you from the present (where your power is) and project you into the future.

If you entertain your fear, if you do not pause, if you do not laugh or at least smile to lighten up and loosen the grip of your fear, your fear will hijack you. Adrenaline will surge through your bloodstream, and you will act out in the way you usually do or play the "what if" game in your head and become very anxious and scared . . . the drama begins yet again. And you freeze.

You can stop the neurochemical release of these neurotransmitters before the hijack occurs. Don't let fear take charge. Stay in the moment, and your fear will dissipate.

Then you can consider what is going on at this moment that requires your attention. Remember, fear, like any emotion, sends you a message. Is it real fear? Is there something you need to do to protect yourself? If not, what is your fear all about? Name your fear so you can reclaim your power and consciously choose your response.

Control What You Can; Let Go of Everything Else

The Law of Attraction teaches us how to tap into synchronicity and the flow of life. Do what you need to do, practice being your best self, and continue to improve and develop yourself, and then things will easily and quite naturally come together for you. As you do for yourself and believe in the possibility of your success, life forces will support your efforts. You will be supported in ways you could not have imagined. Your job is to be open to change and to accept new opportunities as doors open for you. Help yourself and you will be helped—if you are open to receive the gifts.

This is where you have control and possess the greatest power to impact your world. You control *you*—your thoughts and emotions, your behavior, and your choices.

We think we have control over many things, and we hold on very tightly. We spend so much time and effort trying to change things that we have no control over. This causes struggle, and we wish things could be easier. If we let go, however, and focus our attention on what we can control (ourselves), then we experience much less stress and actually gain much more control.

In recovery, they say the serenity prayer on a regular basis. It is a good mantra for each of us (even if you don't normally pray):

> *"God, grant me the serenity to accept the things I cannot change, the courage to change the things I can, and the wisdom to know the difference."*

> —*Reinhold Niebuhr*

If you do what you need to do in this moment, if you allow yourself to enjoy whatever you are doing, then you can let the future take care of itself. Each day you respect yourself and enjoy the choices you make. Each day you become a better you, growing and learning and teaching. Then you can let go and trust that things will work out just the way they should—the way they are supposed to—while you focus attention on enjoying and living your best life today.

You don't have to fight reality.

If you succumb to the resistance and do not do what you need to do, if you do not honor and respect yourself, then you hurt yourself. You lose time and are not living fully or enjoying each day as it is presented to you. Your fear increases as you notice the years passing you by. You will fear death as it approaches because you will have regrets. You will not be ready when your time comes.

If you have a poor track record, then self-trust may not come easy to you. Every time you respect yourself and make good choices on your own behalf, you learn to trust again. As your trust grows, your fear diminishes.

There is nothing to fear when you have faith. This does not mean you need to be religious. This is about trusting you. If you do what you need to do for yourself, if you do the work to improve yourself, then you have nothing to fear. The future is being created with your actions of today.

"Catch" Some Happiness

Consider your vision for how you want to live and enjoy your life. Consider the feelings you wish to enjoy. In your vision, how do you want to feel when you have achieved the result you seek? Envision what you'll be doing and who you might be with. How will it feel to live as you envision?

If you dream of becoming a leader and advancing in your career, how will you feel when you achieve that result? Will you feel happy and confident or worried about whether people will like you, what others will think of you, or if you have what it takes to lead a team? Will you be enjoying your home life, relationships, and hobbies or will you be at the office more than your home? If you dream of being healthier and more physically fit, will you be concerned about the attention you may receive from others? Will you be worried about what your family and friends think of the new you? Or will you be comfortable and confident in your body?

It's important to consider how you want to feel as part of your vision because thoughts coupled with emotions are more potent and powerful. If each day you agonize over making decisions, over whether you have what it takes to succeed, if you're worrying about failing or what others think of you, doubting yourself, and questioning how you will ever get to your goal, then you are getting in your own way by creating obstacles that make it hard if not impossible to overcome. They are impossible because you are creating an inner environment that is negative and self-sabotaging.

What you think about you bring about.

Your inner environment includes your internal dialogue, what you say to yourself all day long. Creating an inner environment that is nurturing and supportive is essential for success. It includes character development (strategy 3), is nurtured by a healthy community of supporters (strategy 4), and is increased as you acknowledge and marvel over how wonderful you are (strategy 6)!

Life is meant to be enjoyed and savored. Life is so fragile, so fleeting. One moment you're here, the next things change. I learned this lesson when first husband died unexpectedly at age 43. Enjoy today. Smile more. Laugh at yourself when you get stuck in your own head. Be with the people you love—really be with them—because tomorrow, they may be busy, or they may be gone.

The other night, our kids wanted to watch a movie that was just released. They were all very excited. I was in the middle of this book project and was very singularly focused. When I saw them all in front of the television, however, I stopped and packed up the computer for the day. I didn't want to miss out on the time to be with my family. Our kids are teenagers. Soon enough, they will be off pursuing their dreams. Today, they are here with us.

No matter what you are doing at any given moment, give yourself the power to choose how to spend your time. Trade every moment for something of value. You can enjoy even the most menial tasks if you can find value in doing them. Why do it if it has no value? That doesn't make much sense. Find value, smile, and enjoy it. It's your choice to use your time in this way. If you are not having fun, then why are you doing it? Find a good reason and hold on to that. This way you can enjoy doing it for that reason. If you don't enjoy your work, for example, but you cannot find a new job yet, you can appreciate this job because it gives you the opportunity to earn a living to support yourself and your family. Enjoy being a breadwinner and a provider. That has great value.

Learning to be happy may be new for some people. It requires being in the present, rather than focusing on what you could be doing or should be doing. It requires letting go of anger or hostility because that keeps you focused on the past and keeps you from enjoying the present. When you lose this moment, you give away the time of your life; time which you cannot retrieve. It's gone. Life is fleeting! Don't lose a moment on petty nonsense, don't waste time stressing over little things that don't matter in the scheme of things, and don't do things that have no value to you. Find value in them or stop doing them.

Learning to be happy means enjoying people, accepting them, and loving them as they are rather than judging; letting go of attachments rather than holding on to things that no longer bring you value or joy; paying attention to what is right in front of you rather than focusing on things over which you have no control; and choosing peace over drama.

By learning to enjoy each moment, you lessen your fear. Fear no longer becomes as important as whatever you choose to enjoy in the moment. You stop entertaining the fear, and it loses its potency. When you focus on being happy and having fun in the moment, you start to make better choices about how to spend your time. You stop doing things that are unhealthy or draining for you, which frees up time for things that you enjoy doing. You will want to do more of the things you enjoy, and you'll have less time for things that you don't.

Happiness then grows.

Laugh along the way because as you laugh, you drink in the moment. If you cannot take pleasure in what you have now, how will you be happy with more? If you do not appreciate where you are on your journey, how will you appreciate it when you are further along the path? You won't ever arrive at happiness because it is not a destination; it is a way of being. You learn to be happy today because today is what you have. You do the very best you can, you give life all you have to give, and, if you should be so blessed to have yet another day tomorrow, you enjoy that day too.

This is how happiness is sowed and reaped: appreciate what you have and where you are on your journey, be grateful for all that you are able to contribute to the lives of others and to the world, laugh so you know you're alive and living well, and always do your best.

Laugh and have fun! If you are having fun, you will keep doing it, and success will be yours.

Easy!

CHAPTER 14

STRATEGY 8:
ADOPT EMPOWERING BELIEFS

---

*"Aerodynamically the bumblebee shouldn't be able to fly,
but the bumblebee doesn't know that, so it goes
on flying anyway."*

—Mary Kay Ash

Beliefs Create Reality

We have discussed your vision for success and the importance of commitment and celebrating your success. We discussed laughter and enjoying the journey. If you're not having fun, why do it? You now know you need to take action and create both an internal and external environment to support and nurture your growth and your success. The final piece is belief; you need to believe that success is not only possible but that you can do it. Strategy 1 regarding commitment says you will go to any and all lengths; this strategy says, "Yes I can!"

If you do not believe you can, then you won't.

Beliefs are your power source. They guide your behaviors, often from behind a curtain. You may not realize what your beliefs are, but they run your life anyway. These are the thoughts behind your habits. The only reason to consciously choose to behave in a certain way is because you believe something about that action. There is value to it, otherwise you would choose something else.

If you are not happy with some result, if the outcome you seek is elusive, check in on your beliefs. Do you believe that what you want is possible for you? What do you believe about this situation, this outcome, this process, and the likelihood of success?

Under a stream or flowing channel of water, there is an undercurrent. It is constant and pervasive, and it moves the water along the channel or canal. So it is with your beliefs. Your beliefs are the undercurrent operating in the background, often subtle, but sometimes very loud.

Beliefs are formed over time; some were formed long ago when you were a child. You learned how to think about and approach life and created an operating system. You heard and saw things that you interpreted to mean something to you and adopted them as yours. You received messages about life and people and emotions, and these created the beliefs that run your life today.

You learned about relationships and how people interact. You learned how to feel about yourself. You learned that you are beautiful (or not) or that you are capable (or not). You learned to struggle for attention. You learned perhaps that life is hard "and then you die." You learned that you are smart and special or that nothing you do is good enough. These beliefs then run your life, and you create a reality to reflect them.

The messages I received growing up led to the belief that nothing I did was good enough, that I was not good enough, and those beliefs show up in my life in many ways. In some ways this was helpful; I was driven to accomplish many things. But it's not helpful if I cannot celebrate my accomplishments or acknowledge how I am good, if it is never enough. I do my best to pay attention to what is driving or motivating me today, to notice when those beliefs are fueling my behaviors so that I can adjust. I have also learned ways to celebrate my success along the way, to hear from others when they offer praise and acknowledgment for my work—something I did not receive much of in my formative years. This message of not being good enough—not doing enough—still shows up, even after all these years, but I am better at noticing it, managing it, and offering myself grace.

What were some of the messages you heard growing up? It's important to identify them; it is also important to suspend judgment. You may find yourself blaming your parents or other adults for instilling these beliefs through their careless messages. Their intention could have been quite different than your interpretation. They may have had no idea of the impact their words would have. People do lots of things without awareness of the impact they have on others.

Focus on what you can control. You can only control today and how you choose to live now. You cannot change the past or hope for a better past. Identify the beliefs so you can challenge them, and then choose empowering new ones to live by.

Beliefs are pervasive habits of thought often wrapped in emotions. You can become attached to your beliefs. Your beliefs are why you keep repeating patterns in your life. Your beliefs are why you are unhappy and why you've been unlucky in certain areas of your life. In fact, whether you believe you are lucky or not is a pervasive thought pattern. If you are not achieving the success you desire, check in on your beliefs.

Hard or easy, it's how you think about it.

Whether something is hard or easy is your perception. If you believe it's hard or believe it's easy, you're right! Your perception fuels your beliefs, and your actions then support those beliefs. In other words, you will behave in ways that support your belief system, to make it true. The result then reinforces your beliefs and your reasons for believing them. In this way, your beliefs create your reality. This is known as confirmation bias.

Everything you do, as well as your values and priorities, are grounded in your beliefs. They create your operating system. If you believe that something is going to be difficult and that you will struggle, then you will create that reality for yourself. It's as if you have set the intention for struggle so you experience struggle. You create stress and drama and, in essence, prove yourself right.

This is a creative form of self-sabotage.

If you believe that the journey will be easy, then you will find ways to make it easy. There will be no struggle, synchronicity will occur, resources will appear, and everything will fall into place—so long as you do the work. You know that you'll face hiccups along the way, yet you approach them with grace and gratitude, trusting that you have the fortitude to get through whatever shows up and that any lessons are there to assist you in your growth and development. You also know that fear will show up and so you expect its appearance. You prepare by nurturing faith in yourself and in your belief in your success to lessen its influence when it appears.

Working against your internal belief system is a losing proposition; you cannot possibly win. You will not commit—you won't be able to—or you will say you are committed, do some of the work, and then sabotage yourself before you reach the finish line to prove yourself right.

You cannot succeed if you honestly and wholeheartedly do not believe in yourself or your dream. It cannot happen. You won't let it. You will not do the work because you don't believe in the possibility for success. You may even beat yourself up for your lack of progress. I mean, really, why bother if you don't believe success is possible? That is a stressful endeavor. You would do better focusing your efforts elsewhere or working to adopt new beliefs.

Use your belief system to assist you with your efforts. Beliefs fuel your desire. They motivate and inspire you to act. When you believe and are committed, you will move mountains—one rock at a time. But if you do not believe it, all your efforts will be in vain.

Choose Empowering Beliefs

You are embarking on a new journey. No matter how many times you may have tried before and not achieved the results you desired, this time is new. You are new, and you now have strategies to assist you along the way. You have a plan, and you need your beliefs to support you. Because beliefs are the undercurrent of your life, they are very powerful. You need them to be on your side.

What are some of the things you believe now about your quest? Let's get them out in the open. Your beliefs will be wrapped up in the explanations or stories you tell about why your circumstances or experiences are as they are. Once you identify your beliefs, you can challenge them and choose new, more appropriate, empowering beliefs to help you on your journey. You are in charge of your beliefs!

Why do you keep choosing the wrong mate or job? What are you looking for? What are your expectations? Is there something you are doing to sabotage your success in some way? Get honest with yourself.

Why might you always seem to clash with your boss or coworkers? Is it true that other people are the problem or is it possible, since you are the constant in these situations, that something you are doing is creating this difficulty?

Why do you struggle with overwhelm and anxiety? Why do you find yourself doing more work than is possible for you to do? What beliefs do you harbor about saying yes to requests? What is your struggle with saying no or with delegating tasks to your teammates?

Why do you keep finding yourself in debt? Listen to how you talk about and treat your money. What do you believe about money or debt? Do you tend to make purchases based on need or want? How does spending money make you feel? Do you make excuses for your situation or for your spending patterns? Is there a self-esteem issue here that needs to be addressed?

Why do you not lose weight and keep it off? Why do you seem to practice yo-yo dieting? What are your thoughts about food? How do you feel about your body? What gets in the way of envisioning yourself healthier and maintaining that vision? Do you feel you are not worthy? What do you believe about your ability to lose weight and to maintain a smaller body? Do you think it is possible? What do you value—not what you think you should value, but what value reflects the way you live now?

Often the first answer is a superficial one. Do not let yourself off the hook that easily! Ask yourself more questions until you get to the reason for behaving as you do. What do you believe about this situation or person?

Do not judge your responses. Some may seem silly or not make much sense. Remember that some of your beliefs were formed when you were very young. They are still running your life because you have not yet explored them and updated them. The person you were when you cultivated the belief is not the person you are today. You have changed. So must your beliefs, which is why this exercise is essential.

Once you uncover the belief, you can choose a new one. The belief that has been running your life is old and outdated; it does not bring you the results you seek. Choose a new belief—a new thought—that will empower you and add value to your life.

Nurture this new thought so that it can become a habit. Each time you reinforce this thought you create and strengthen the neurological connections associated with the idea. Eventually, it becomes habit, and you act automatically based on this belief.

Be careful how you introduce a new belief. You cannot change a belief; you have to replace it. The mind operates in a certain way. If you fight with your thoughts, then you actually strengthen the neurological connections you want to eliminate.

For instance, you want to lose weight. Based on past experience, you believe it won't happen. You've tried to lose weight before, but you give up after a short time. You uncover that the way you sabotage is you don't follow through, you are scared of receiving the attention that being thinner will bring you, you think it's just too much work, it requires too much of you, and you don't have the time. The same thing could be said if you wanted to make any kind of change: you have tried this before, it's too much work, and you'll never get it right or be successful.

Now you entertain thoughts of changing your eating habits yet again. You want to be healthy, and changing your nutrition is one way you can start on that path. But the first thing that happens—in your mind—is a battle of your beliefs. *You can't lose weight! Yes, I can! If I work really hard, I will! No, you can't. Yes, I can! No, you can't. Yes, I can.*

There are no winners in this argument. What essentially happens is that you reinforce the notion that you have been unsuccessful in the past while at the same time trying to convince yourself that this time will be different.

Instead of trying to convince yourself of anything, just adopt a new belief. It is different this time. You are different. It is a new day. You are embarking upon a new life. You have new tools and new strategies. The past is a wonderful reference for learning how *not* to do something. There are rich lessons there for you to learn from. The past does not have to dictate your future.

Og Mandino said it best in his perennial best seller, *The Greatest Salesman in the World*, when he stated,

> As a child I was slave to my impulses; now I am slave to my habits, as are all grown men. I have surrendered my free will to the years of accumulated habits and the past deeds of my life have already marked out a path which threatens to imprison my future. My actions are ruled by appetite, passion, prejudice, greed, love, fear, environment, habit, and the worst of these tyrants is habit. Therefore, if I must be a slave to habit let me be a slave to good habits.

You control your thoughts by observing them. When you think a thought and uncover a belief, question it. Does it add value? Does this belief system move you toward the happiness and success you desire? If not, what thought can you choose that will better aid you on your journey?

You may have to look for new thoughts and perspectives. This is why having a support system is helpful. Spending time with other people who are traveling the same path immerses you in an environment that introduces you to new thoughts and ideas and provides you with the frame of mind needed for success in your particular endeavor. A professional coach helps you to explore your thinking and the underlying beliefs. You then have the opportunity to adopt new beliefs and create habits of thought that provide the undercurrent that will lead you to the outcome you desire.

No You Can't!

Let's go back in time to when you were a child. Take a moment to consider the messages you heard growing up. Your mother or father told you, "No you can't." Your sibling said, "You're so stupid!" Perhaps you were bullied as a kid. What were the messages that you heard?

Perhaps you were not told anything explicitly, but there were silent expectations that you would behave a certain way, hold a particular job, play a particular sport, etc. How did that affect you growing up, and what are the beliefs you hold today because of these expectations?

You heard many messages in your youth about what you could and could not do and who you should be. At the moment when you heard the message, you began to have thoughts that shape and question who you are to become. These sneaky, pervasive thoughts start to hum in the background of your mind: *You can't. Who do you think you are to want that? Women can't . . . Men don't . . . You shouldn't. You're not smart enough, good enough, ____ enough. It's not possible. You'll never . . .*

Unfortunately, you create neurological connections that strengthen this belief each and every time you think the thought.

This creates a habit of thought that becomes the undercurrent of your life. You act accordingly and create in reality the very thing that you didn't want. You succumb to these habits of thought and become a slave to them.

There are definitive words that cue you to the presence of a limiting belief. These include words such as *can't*, *won't*, *never*, and *always*. Listen to yourself as you speak, especially about your goal. What do you say or think about it?

Limiting beliefs hold you back from achieving success because they do not let you see the likelihood of it. These definitive words cause you to shut the door on possibility. Consider, for example, the statement *I can never save money.* This statement means that you are convinced that there is no hope. There is no possibility of success; therefore, you won't bother to do anything about it.

I always choose the wrong mate. This means that you do not make good decisions about relationships. It implies that you never make a good decision.

But that's not true, is it? You do sometimes make good decisions. Limiting beliefs are ideas that often lack the truth to back them up. Unless you stop to notice them, and challenge them, you live as if they are truth and create a life that supports them.

I never get promoted. Have you done the work necessary to obtain the promotion or have you simply hoped for it? What is the message here for you? There is a lesson for you to learn, a blind spot you are not seeing, or a wall that you are hitting—you may need to change directions (or change companies).

Listen for these limiting words or phrases whether you say them out loud or think them to yourself. Often, it is what happens in the privacy of our minds that hurts us the most.

If you hear yourself say or think a limiting belief, change the statement to include the word *yet*. *I have yet to meet the love of my life. I have yet to be promoted. I have not yet learned how to delegate or say no to new tasks to reduce my overwhelm. I have not yet lost this weight.* Then, you can choose to envision a new life and commit to it—or not. At least you are in charge of making the decision.

Your beliefs are so important that you must take really good care of them. Nurture those that are empowering and positive and that add value and support you in achieving your dreams. Beliefs are part of your inner environment. Focus on the characteristics required for success in this endeavor. What are some of the beliefs that will be necessary to achieve the success you desire? Consider the people who have what you desire; what do they believe?

If unhappiness, stress, doubt, and negative self-esteem are learned through the consistent repetition of thoughts doused with emotion, then so are happiness, peace, well-being, and positive self-esteem.

What If You Can?

What if it is possible to have what you want? What if it is possible to find love after all these years being single? What if you can get promoted or move to a new company? What if you can be successful running your own business? What if just maybe you could earn more money, take that big vacation, lose that weight, or quit smoking (or some other bad habit) once and for all?

What if?

Embracing possibility means opening your mind to the possibility that the story you have been telling yourself all this time could be flawed. Perhaps the story is not the whole truth. Perhaps you are missing something that you did not realize you were missing.

It is difficult to admit defeat. It is difficult to admit that you could be wrong. We don't want to hear that! Possibility thinking means that there is another way. It does not assume or judge your way as being wrong or bad; it merely suggests that there is another way possible. Your way works to get you *here*; in this way, you were right. But in order to get where you want to go, you need to discover new ways of thinking, and you need new beliefs to guide you.

By embracing possibility, you loosen the grip of your current thinking that you cannot do something or that it is not possible. "Cannot" is a limiting belief. Limiting beliefs close doors and create barriers or ceilings to success and happiness.

When you ask "What if?" even if you don't believe it now, your subconscious starts to wonder. The words are whirling around upstairs in your mind trying to find an opening, a window, a flaw in your perfectly crafted ideas about how life is.

What if there is a better way to think or to approach something? Is it possible that your life could be different? Is it possible that you could accomplish this goal? Other people have achieved similar success. How might you do it too?

Consider the possibility that you could achieve your goal. Notice your thoughts as they struggle to consider alternatives or possibilities. What are you thinking? What are you feeling? Check in with your body. Is there a sensation somewhere in your body, perhaps in your gut or your chest? You don't have to do anything; just notice the thoughts and notice the feelings or sensations. Awareness is empowering.

If you feel fear, laugh and it will diminish. Fear limits you and narrows your thinking. Laughter opens up possibilities as you shrink fear down to size. What if you really can have what you want? Imagine the possibilities . . .

Set an Intention for Success

Commitment makes the statement that you are doing whatever it takes. You are going for this goal, and you will make it happen! Believing means you have the faith and confidence that you will succeed.

Belief is an attitude. Set your intention to succeed and carry that thought process with you. It is going to happen; it is just a matter of time and of doing the work required. You will become a new person with the right characteristics necessary to achieve your goal. This faith and trust carry you through to the next step on the journey.

When change occurs, you lose your footing. Everything you know is shaken up. There is a sense of loss. You mourn, even if you have been unhappy and are now glad for change to take place. The future is unclear; even if you have a strong vision to guide your way, it is still a fantasy, a thought, an idea. It is not reality yet.

You may question the possibility of success. You may question your ability, your knowledge, or your skills. You may question your deservedness. Self-esteem can certainly get in the way.

Belief is what carries you through. Belief causes you to move forward without hesitation and take that next step. It is the driving force for your progress.

To believe means that you expect success. You set an intention for your vision to become reality—eventually—and trust that the answers will come to you as you need them, the right resources or people will enter your life as you need them, and the best outcome will result—perhaps even greater than you anticipated or envisioned. You focus on doing the work and taking action. Control what you can and let go of trying to control the outcome and things over which you have no control. There is no struggle. You have faith that the actions you are taking are the right actions and, so long as you persist, you will succeed.

Discouragement is a test of your faith and belief. What is being asked of you is to recommit to your vision and take another step. Acknowledge just how far you have come and realize that success takes as long as it takes.

Trust that life is unfolding as it should. Trust that you will achieve the success you desire if you take another step in the direction of your dreams. And trust that if you do what is in your best interest, if you do the right thing for you, then you will be supported and all you need will be provided.

The Law of Attraction tells us that if we focus on developing our "attractiveness" and doing the right things, we will become a magnet for what we desire. Why not expect synchronicity to occur on your journey? If you do the work, take the action steps, develop your character, and create a healthy external environment to support you, why would you not expect success to occur? It may not occur at the pace you wish it would, but that is about you, your expectations, and your judgment of timing.

It will happen; you just don't know when. Be patient and nurture your belief in success.

Believe in You

Believe that you can. Believe that you will. Believe that you deserve and are worthy of success. Do not allow self-esteem issues or bad habits of thought to hold you back from achieving your dream and experiencing the happiness you desire. You have the right to success. You are competent and capable. You have a track record for success in other areas of your life. Develop your confidence by being more committed to change than you are to your fear. Rise above your resistance by taking baby steps.

You are amazing and deserve all of the happiness you can "catch" for yourself!

CHAPTER 15

CONCLUSION

"Nothing splendid has ever been achieved except by those who dared believe that something inside of them was superior to circumstance."

—Bruce Barton

The Strategies in Practice

Change is hard, but with these eight strategies, you can learn to make it easy to embark upon a personal change and succeed with less effort, struggle, and stress. If you want to change, you'll need to know why: Why is this change important for you? What is important about this change, and why now? This will help motivate you through to the finish line.

The strategies are numbered to provide order so that they can be presented to you. And while it may be that as you practice them, you find that there is an order in which you prefer to use them, there may be no particular order in practice.

You may find that the community comes first. For example, you decide to take on a new workout class. There, you meet new people, and they value their health differently by working out regularly and eating more nutritionally. This is attractive to you and motivates you to embark upon a personal change, so you, too, begin to value your health differently and take new actions. This inspires you to envision something new for yourself, and the rest of the strategies then fall in line.

You may find that vision comes first and then you commit, set up your environment, and take action. A client recently expressed her desire to begin a blog to help share her knowledge and be seen as an expert in her field. She had the vision for quite some time and set up a plan of action with a list of steps; however, she did not have the drive or commitment to get started. Other priorities kept getting in her way. When we discussed this, she determined that what she needed was some level of accountability to inspire her to act. This enabled her to commit to a timeline and set some deadlines for launching the blog. For this client, setting up the environment of support was necessary for taking the required action.

Wherever it begins, all the strategies are necessary for success.

- Laughter helps you to enjoy the process and keeps you from being too serious.

- Empowering beliefs enable you to take the next step and the next and the next.

- Your vision keeps you focused on your destination.

- Commitment keeps you focused on your vision and taking the next step so you do not veer off course. It helps you to persist.

- Action keeps fear at a minimum.

- Celebrating along the way keeps you from getting discouraged as you take the steps necessary to climb your staircase to success.

- Having a community of supporters keeps you motivated and engaged in the process.

- Along the way, you develop your character, which helps you to gain confidence and faith and affords you the ability to sustain the success you achieve.

There is no right or wrong way to practice. As emotions emerge— and they will—be open to exploring them. Let go of what was; do not be attached to people, places, or things. Allow space for new people, places, and things to enter your life. Trust that new things will present themselves for you to enjoy and have faith that the resources you need will emerge as you need them.

Change is hard. Use these strategies to help you to succeed and to make the changes you need in order to enjoy yourself and your life. Don't let fear win. Face your fear, remembering that you are in charge. You are in control of your thoughts as well as your emotional responses. Be willing to explore any resistance you feel. Be at choice. This is where your power is.

Check your expectations along the way and watch for signs of discouragement. You are quite amazing, and it will be important for your success to acknowledge and celebrate all you do as you walk the staircase to success. Keep taking another step and stay committed to your goal. Believe that success is possible. With commitment, it is.

A New Life Begins

You decide to embark upon change. You envision yourself doing something else and enjoying a new experience in life. Whether you had an awakening (a "whack" on the side of your head) or simply decided it was time, you are motivated and ready to commit to this change. You want something different. Congratulations!

Nowhere in this book have I said you will not have to work. Change requires work. You will need to do things differently and be open to exploring new possibilities. You need to lighten up and let go of things that were previously comfortable for you in order to make space for something new. Change can be uncomfortable. Although you may mourn the past, enjoy taking new steps today, and look ahead at the future with anticipation, excitement, and an open heart.

Commit to making a change. Commit to doing anything and everything it takes to achieve your goal. There is no turning back. Close the door behind you.

Envision what you want with specific detail and emotion. Nurture this vision in your mind. Write it down on paper. Read it daily and add to it when the vision becomes clearer. Create a collage if you like and post it where you can see it daily.

Celebrate your success and acknowledge the actions steps you take. Look how far you have come and how you have changed in the process. Do not worry over things beyond your control. Do not entertain negative thoughts. Question your expectations and recognize that there is a pace to life. Time cannot be rushed. It has its own schedule. Trust that you will be prepared when the time comes. Live in this moment and do what you can. This is what you have control of.

Recognize your fear when it rears its ugly head and laugh. Lighten up at the silly things you hold tight to. Loosen the grip. There is very little of such great importance that will not be forgotten ten years from now. At the end of the day, consider what is of greatest value to you. Is holding on to a particular idea really so important?

Learn to laugh and enjoy the journey. Happiness is not a destination; it is a state of being. Stop and watch the sunset. Enjoy your children while you can; you'll enjoy the empty house when they are gone. And you'll miss them. Enjoy the changing of the seasons. Enjoy the disoriented feeling of being in the middle of change. Enjoy yourself today because tomorrow today will be gone.

Take action to achieve your goals. Without action, nothing changes. Everything in your life stays the same until you take a little step in the direction of your dream; one step, then another and another. With each baby step, you gain momentum. You fuel your commitment.

Acknowledge the steps you take so you don't fall victim to discouragement. Small steps produce big results. Keep taking another step until you achieve your goal.

Develop the characteristics of someone who has the results you desire. How do they think? What do they value? Nurture an inner environment that supports you in developing the attributes you need to take you in the direction you wish to go. In this way, you ensure that you will sustain the change you wish to make because you will have developed your character. Watch your inner dialogue. Tell yourself only positive and uplifting things. You deserve to be treated with respect. Start by treating yourself with respect—in your own mind.

Create an external environment that will support your success. Change your physical environment to suit your needs and create a community or hire a coach that will support, motivate, and inspire you, teach you what you need to know, and expand your perspective. You can learn from the mistakes of others and mentor others along the way. You are not alone. Having support increases the probability for success. You need someone who believes in you, who celebrates your successes with you, and who holds you up when you experience defeat. Learn to ask others for help when you need it and put strong boundaries in place with those in your life who may not be supportive.

Believe you can. Believe with every fiber of your being that you will achieve your goal. If you do what you need to do to respect yourself, then you will receive the support you need in the form of resources, ideas, teachers, and other synchronistic events. You have the right to be happy and achieve all the success you desire. You, however, have to pursue your own happiness.

Whatever you want for yourself, I want that for you. I hope this book inspires you to make the changes you desire for yourself and your happiness. Let me know how these strategies are helping you. And if you are struggling, I want to know that too.

Visit me at www.DrJulieDonley.com. I look forward to hearing from you. There is no reason to struggle lest you fall victim to the tricks of your mind. With these strategies, you have the tools to help you play this game and win. Now go create the success and happiness you long for.

Enjoy your journey!

GRATITUDE

Community and support are so important for accomplishing our goals and, in writing this book, there were several people whose contributions were essential for its success.

Writing a book is a huge endeavor. It is a labor of love and a place where I find *flow*, so I can become very committed and single-focused when I am involved in a writing project. I am grateful to my family for their unwavering support and encouragement. I am so very grateful for my husband, Lou, who is my rock and a huge supporter. I am grateful for my sister, Lori Reichner, who keeps me on track and always has my back. Our children are big fans of my work; one of my sons even distributes my books to colleagues at work. And I thank my parents who, in their own way, have provided me with the inspiration to keep learning and growing.

I am grateful for fellow coach Teresa Smith and business coach Karyn Greenstreet who, at the original writing of this text, encouraged and supported me to complete the manuscript.

Much gratitude goes to friends, clients, colleagues—all the people over the years who have encouraged me to continue to write the books that are living in my head!

I am thankful for Geoff Affleck and his team for their work in republishing this book, and for Elizabeth Thorlton who provided the editing services.

I am very grateful for my coaching and leadership development clients from whom I learn so much. It is an honor and privilege to witness the amazing transformation that occurs when greatness emerges and change takes place—when they reach a new "step" on their staircase to success, honor themselves in a new way, or find the happiness that has eluded them.

For this and more, I am forever grateful.

ABOUT DR. JULIE DONLEY

Dr. **Julie Donley** is a leadership expert, professional certified coach, and award-winning author known for helping leaders reduce stress, communicate with clarity, and lead with confidence and calm. Her clients describe her work as life-changing—transforming how they lead, communicate, and strengthen relationships. She is deeply dedicated to bringing out the best in people and creating workplaces where everyone can thrive.

Julie's passion for leadership was sparked early in her healthcare career, when she witnessed the damaging effects of toxic leadership on teams and patient care. That experience led to decades of study and practice focused on people-centered leadership. She later served as a director of nursing in behavioral health, deepening her understanding of what it takes to lead effectively in high-stakes environments.

Her doctoral research explored how psychosocial work environments affect job satisfaction in behavioral healthcare, reinforcing her commitment to respectful, trust-based leadership. Julie holds advanced degrees in organizational leadership, business, and nursing, and is widely recognized for her contributions to leadership development.

She lives in Pennsylvania with her husband, Lou. They enjoy traveling—often by motorcycle—and listening to the Grateful Dead.

Learn more at DrJulieDonley.com.

ALSO BY DR. JULIE DONLEY

The Journey Called You

Embark on a journey into the world of self-awareness and self-wonder. Discover yourself,, get to know yourself better, learn to accept yourself without judgment, and make decisions that honor the highest form of you. In the end you feel more confident and grounded in yourself so you can create your life, day-by-day, feeling good about who you are, the choices you make, and the life you live.

Leading at the Speed of People

Unlock the secrets to transformative leadership that puts people first, reduces stress, and drives unparalleled results. Leading at the Speed of People presents a transformative approach to leadership that drives impactful results by prioritizing empathy and respect. This engaging and action-oriented guide provides practical strategies for connecting deeply with your team, reducing workplace stress, and achieving remarkable outcomes.

Thank you for reading my book. The best way to help this work reach others is to leave a short book review. Please go to Amazon and leave a review here: amazon.com/review/create-review/?&asin=B0CGVS32BB

THE STRATEGIES IN REVIEW

Strategy 1: *Commit to change.* If you are not happy with something in your life, decide to change. If you want something better for yourself, commit to change. By committing, you take a stand for you and your happiness. You elevate yourself in importance in your life. By committing, you shift internally. You become willing to learn what you need to do differently in order to produce a new result. You cannot behave the same way and produce something new. You have to learn new things.

Strategy 2: *Envision a better future.* Close your eyes and envision the change you desire. It can be any change, such as an improved relationship with your parent or a colleague or your spouse. It can be moving across the country, getting a promotion, writing a novel, or planning for retirement. Your vision is the beacon of light that shines the way. Commitment solidifies the direction you are resigned to traveling in your vision.

Strategy 3: *Develop the characteristics you need to succeed.* "Be the change." Become the kind of person who would have what you desire. Identify and then develop the qualities that you envision yourself portraying in your vision. You are different in your vision for the future. How are you different? Look at how confident, dependable, and trustworthy you are. What is important to you in your future vision? Start developing these qualities now. Live them today.

Strategy 4: ***Create an environment to support the change.*** Arrange your environment to assist you in developing these characteristics, in taking the required actions, and in teaching you new ideas and new behaviors. If you want to be different, you must behave differently. Do not rely solely on yourself; this is self-sabotaging. There are people in your life today that may resist the change you want to make. Be prepared to extend strong boundaries. There are things you are accustomed to that will not serve you in making this change. Learn to let go and move on. Your environment is crucial for nurturing you as you develop, evolve, and become someone new.

Strategy 5: ***Take action.*** Without action, nothing changes. Take one small step. Then take another. And another. Before you know it, you will have gained momentum. Have fun taking new steps and remember that success comes in stages. It doesn't happen all at once but rather with small changes over time. *Small steps produce big results.*

Strategy 6: ***Celebrate your success along the way.*** When you acknowledge the steps you've taken and the progress you've made, you increase your confidence and strengthen the beliefs you have in the possibility for success. By celebrating your progress, you diminish the possibility for discouragement. You also improve your ability to make realistic expectations or better guesses for how quickly you can accomplish the results you seek. Change takes time, and while you may not be where you want to be, by acknowledging where you are along the journey, you recognize that you are no longer where you were, and you see just how far you have come.

Strategy 7: *Laugh and enjoy the journey.* Laughter helps you keep things in perspective. It also helps you enjoy yourself and be happy. Laughter keeps your wall down too. It is hard to hide when you are having fun—and you don't want to! Surround yourself with people who make you laugh and stay away from negativity and drama. Life is too short. Savor every moment.

Strategy 8: *Adopt empowering beliefs.* Your beliefs are the undercurrent for everything you do. When they are limiting, you succumb to self-sabotaging and avoidance behaviors. Limiting beliefs are grounded in fear. Be aware of the words you choose. Expose your limiting beliefs and start shifting them to empowering ones. You have not *yet* accomplished this goal. You have not *yet* achieved success, even though you may have tried before. You have not *yet*, but you will now!

APPENDIX II

RESOURCES

Allen, D. (2002). *Getting things done: The art of stress-free productivity.* Piatkus Books.

Bradberry, T., & Greaves, J. (2009). *Emotional Intelligence 2.0.* TalentSmart.

Bridges, W. (2017). *Managing transitions: Making the most of change.* Da Capo Lifelong Books.

Covey, S. (1989). *The seven habits of highly effective people.* Simon and Schuster.

Donley, J. (2005). *The journey called you: A roadmap to self-discovery and acceptance.* Nurturing Your Success LLC.

Hartman, R. (2011). *The structure of value.* Wipf & Stock.

Jeffers, S. (2007). *Feel the fear and do it anyway.* Vermilion.

Kübler-Ross, E. (1970). *On death and dying.* Collier Books/Macmillan Publishing Co.

Kübler-Ross, E., & Kessler, D. (2001). *Life lessons: Two experts on death and dying teach us about the mysteries of life and living.* Scribner.

Mandino, O. (1983). *Greatest salesman in the world.* Bantam.

Maté, D. G. (2018). *In the realm of hungry ghosts.* Vermilion.

Rath, T., & Harter, J. (2010). *Wellbeing: The five essential elements.* Gallup Press.

Ruiz, D. M. (2001). *The four agreements.* Amber-Allen Publishing.

www.ingramcontent.com/pod-product-compliance
Lightning Source LLC
Chambersburg PA
CBHW021716120626
46545CB00004B/1585